REFLECTIVE LIVING:
A SPIRITUAL APPROACH
TO EVERYDAY LIVING

REFLECTIVE LIVING: A SPIRITUAL APPROACH TO EVERYDAY LIVING

CLAIRE M. BRISSETTE

AFFIRMATION BOOKS
WHITINSVILLE, MASSACHUSETTS

For my parents,
Aime and Claire,
whose lives speak profoundly
of lived spiritual values

Published with ecclesiastical permission

First Edition

© 1983 by Claire M. Brissette

Cover and illustrations pages 44 and 120 are photographs of art work by Barbara M. Palicki; page 96 by Barbara Mispilkin.

The quotations on page 102 are excerpted from *Out of Solitude* by Henry J. M. Nouwen. Copyright © 1974 by Ave Maria Press, Notre Dame, Ind. 46556. Used with permission of the publisher.

Library of Congress Cataloging in Publication Data

Brissette, Claire M.
    Reflective living.

    1. Christian life—Catholic authors.   I. Title.
BX2350.2.B7   1983   248.4   83-21369
ISBN 0-89571-019-6

Printed by
Mercantile Printing Company, Worcester, Massachusetts
United States of America

Contents

Foreword

Approaching the year 2000 finds the human community in many frantic races. The arms race, the computer information race, the success race, the race to equality, the daily work race or as the cliche too often states it, "the rat race." Life is meant to be more than just reacting, reacting, and more reacting. For life to be truly free, fully human, it must necessarily take on a reflective element. Reflective behavior holds the power of good physical, emotional, and spiritual health.

Reflective Living by Claire M. Brissette is an invitation to take the reflective aspect of life seriously and she offers several practical suggestions as how best to do so. Affirmation Books is happy to present this book to the general public because it draws upon the insights of theology and psychology, and in combining them arrives at a psychotheological approach. It reflects on the experience of many of the great truths of our Judeo-Christian tradition; it emphasizes the fact that theological truths are essentially intermingled and mutually illuminating.

The first encounter with the term "psychotheological" could evoke the image of some new hybrid science with its own independent subject matter and means of inquiry. However, strictly speaking, psychotheology is not a science but rather an approach to life which draws on secular and religious sources of truth so as to better our response to the total human person as created, redeemed, and called by God in Christ Jesus. This view of the human person is an acknowledgment of the integration of the human and divine which already exists perfectly in Christ and which serves as the inspiring vision, the reassuring reality, the very way to the Father, shared by all Christians on the journey to their own hearts.

It is primarily within the heart of the human person that this integration must begin to take place. The open heart is the only soil in which the Word of God and his grace can take root. God does not work in a vacuum, nor does he say "no" to his own creation. Whatever helps us to find our true hearts and open them to God in experience and in life is good mental health at work. It is also God at work. The integration of the human and the divine which a psychotheological approach to the human person seeks is what Christ seeks.

There is also an integration between psychology and theology at a secondary level that guides us in our attempts to achieve the primary integration in our hearts. This union occurs at the level of knowledge and insight. It must be emphasized that such an integration does not blur the distinction between nature and grace, between the natural and the supernatural, between psychology and theology. Neither does it deny the palpable presence of God in many people who cannot achieve the primary integration referred to above. If anything, it heightens our appreciation of both sources of truth and prompts us to listen more respectfully to God speaking in them by honoring the noblest traditions of each science. The knowledge and insight gained by a dialogue between these areas of God's truth come from the mutual highlighting of areas of human experience produced in turn by both theology and psychology. Each science in its own way provides an increased awareness, an illumination and unraveling of the human experience, in which God speaks and responds to his precious creation, leading especially to personal growth within a family or community setting.

A psychotheological approach to the problems of human living is a source of nourishment for solutions to these problems. If society is to be healed and the identity of each individual is to be assured, there must be an increased awareness of the need for an integrated development in human society: that is, a furthering of the physical, mental, social, and spiritual development of the whole person.

It is my hope that Claire Brissette's *Reflective Living* will challenge your thought and encourage your faith. Taken seriously, this book could assist you in the direction of living life with a new sense of happiness.

> Thomas A. Kane, Ph.D., D.P.S.
> Priest, Diocese of Worcester
> Publisher, Affirmation Books
> Whitinsville, Massachusetts

24 October 1983

Introduction

As I listen each day to people sharing their life experience, I frequently hear the following: "I'm on a merry-go-round"; "My life is a rat race"; "I'm exhausted just running from one thing to another"; "I have to slow down." These and similar descriptions characterize the age in which we live: we are constantly on the move and caught up in activity from morning till night, day after day. Most often the morning alarm sets us in motion for the day. Is it any wonder that we turn off the lights at night feeling exhausted?

To some extent, each of us tends to live in a state of wakeful sleep, more or less consciously going through the motions of our everyday life and experience. Rarely do we take the time to get in touch with and to reflect upon the deeper meanings of our experiences. We tend to feel that such reflection is simply a waste of time.

Yet the potential for reflection is rooted in our nature. Each of us has the ability to touch the deeper meanings of our everyday experience. Through reflection we glimpse something of the mystery of life, and as a consequence our lives are enriched. Daily activity ceases to be monotonous, and reflective dwelling opens our eyes to the wonder hidden in the most insignificant experiences.

I believe that each of us is capable of developing a reflective approach to life. The opportunities to stop, look at, and listen to life are already there, hidden in the rhythm of our daily routine.

This book represents my attempt to raise to the level of conscious awareness the already existing structures for reflective living rooted in the dynamics of our personality and in the rhythm of our ordinary lives. It is addressed to lay and religious women and men desirous of living a richer life.

My interest in this topic has developed gradually. Throughout the past ten years various circumstances have thrown me back on myself and forced me to look at and to listen to my own life. Guided through this reflective process by formal schooling and special individuals, I began to recognize the value of reflection in my own life. Moreover, my ministry in the area of spiritual development has led me to believe that reflection is an essential condition for human and spiritual growth. In these pages, I wish to share the fruit of my experience and my beliefs about a reflective approach to life.

This project is rooted in phenomenology ; that is, I have tried to uncover the basic elements of reflective living already present in the ordinariness of daily life. Focusing on human experience, I have drawn upon the insights of the human sciences and of the spiritual masters insofar as these serve to clarify lived experience.

Each chapter explores a specific aspect of human experience as it relates to developing a reflective attitude. I begin by looking at the nature and meaning of reflection as we experience it each day. I then consider the implications for reflective living of the inevitable embeddedness that dulls us to the meaning of our experience. In chapter three I elaborate on how growing in an awareness of our personal rhythm of presence and distance is an essential element in developing a reflective attitude. I go on to suggest and describe concrete ways of growing into a reflective approach to life by becoming increasingly sensitive to our personal rhythm. After describing the dynamics of our human experience, I then explore the implications for our Christian lives of intimacy with God and service to others.

Sensitive to the issue of sexist language, I have tried to vary the use of masculine and feminine pronouns. In many instances I attempted to use both pronouns side by side. However, consistent use of this method proved to be awkward and distracting. For the same reason I have chosen to retain the biblical image of God as Father. It is my hope that the reader will understand.

I am indebted to Adrian van Kaam, C.S.Sp., Ph.D., and Charles Maes, Ph.D., of the Institute of Formative Spirituality, and to Vincent Bilotta III, Ph.D., of the House of Affirmation, whose thinking has significantly influenced the evolution of my thoughts and the reflective direction of my life. I am appreciative to Martin Helldorfer, F.S.C., whose helpful insights and encouragement have contributed to this book. I am also grateful to the lay and religious groups to whom I have ministered and to the many individuals whom I accompany in their journey of faith. Their sharing, reflections, insights, and questions have helped me to form my own thoughts and have enriched the content of this book.

As you read through these pages may you tap the depths of your own reflective potential and allow yourself to discover and to trust the richness of your ordinary experience. May your life be enriched by your ongoing growth into a reflective attitude.

Claire M. Brissette

Chapter one

Living reflectively

For several years, I had the privilege of living along Newport, Rhode Island's "Cliff Walk" overlooking Easton's Beach and Narragansett Bay. One of my favorite pastimes was strolling along the beach or the Walk, allowing myself to be quieted and filled by the natural beauty. Frequently during those walks, I saw others sitting or standing along the grassy edge of the cliffs, or walking quietly along the beach, looking out at the vastness of the sea and seemingly lost in thought. At times, I was tempted to engage them in conversation, in an effort to discover what drew them to the sea, what called them to be quiet and alone. Their reflective attitude, however, urged me to respect their quiet solitude. I would simply walk by and continue on my way, reverently honoring their wish to remain undisturbed.

As I began to listen to my own reasons for walking the cliffs and the beach alone, and as I listened to friends, I found myself reinforced in my belief that all of us, in varying degrees, need to be alone with ourselves. A friend of mine would faithfully walk the beach each day and "talk to the sea gulls." It was his way of gaining distance from and perspective on the incessant demands of his position as pastor of a large parish. Another friend would unwind at the end of the day, seeking the restorative effect of the vast sea stretched out before her. During the late afternoon and early evening hours, the beach seemed for many the place to be alone and quiet. At the end of a full day, I often found myself saying, "I need to clear my head." Or, when I was working through some inner struggle, I needed "space" or needed to "let things settle." At such times, I was naturally drawn to the cliffs or the beach, where in quiet solitude I found myself spontaneously getting in touch with my inner world of feelings, concerns, preoccupations, and aspirations. During these moments I could allow everything to settle, to be, and to speak to me in its own way. Without any deliberate planning, I was caught up in a reflective moment. I often came away from such moments feeling refreshed and challenged by deeper insight into myself or a situation. At other times, I came away with renewed courage and vigor.

Such experiences reveal the fact that as human beings, embodied spirits, each of us has the ability to reflect. Unlike animals, who instinctively react to the immediate, we can distance ourselves from the immediacy of our everyday life in order to reflect on it. The word "reflect" originates from the Latin *re,* meaning "back," and *flectere,* "to bend." Reflect, then, literally, is "to bend back." Bending back on our experience, re-viewing it within ourselves, can foster new or deeper insight into how we are living, or it may simply provide the necessary time and space to allow thoughts and feelings to settle within us.

This reflection is something we do spontaneously many times each day, in relation to all kinds of experiences, from the insignificant "That walk in the brisk air really refreshed me" to the more personally meaningful "For the first time, I'm realizing that she really cares for me." During such moments, we almost automatically find ourselves thinking over, pondering, or meditating upon what we as unique individuals have experienced. Just as we may look into a mirror to see how well a suit fits or to comb our hair, thus putting it in order, so also do we reflect upon the life we are living to consider the extent to which it does or does not "fit" our unique individuality. At other times, moments of reflection may call us to "put in order," in tune with who we are, certain aspects of our lives. Such moments, then, are a way of getting in touch with our experience in order to evaluate it and integrate its meaning into our lives.

Reflective moments can develop into a reflective way of life. As we grow in the ability to become reflective, we begin to bend back habitually on our lived experience. Such a way of life fosters being present to ourselves. The distance of reflection provides greater objectivity, thus enabling us to place our experience—our feelings, thoughts, projects, plans, encounters—into proper perspective in relationship to our whole life and, ultimately, in relationship to God's unfolding plan for our lives.

Our daily world of responsibilities and obligations constantly calls us out of ourselves. We must be totally present to the work we do each day, to the book we are reading, to the traffic through which we drive. We must also be present to the persons with whom we live and work. We have responsibilities to fulfill; decisions to make; projects to carry out; meals to prepare; appointments to keep. In the midst of everyday busyness, it is relatively easy to become preoccupied and fragmented. We may come to see our various responsibilities as so many isolated compartments of our lives, just so many obligations to fulfill before we can take time to live. As we run busily from one task to another, we risk losing ourselves and consequently bringing to daily responsibilities, as well as to the persons with whom we live and work, an impoverished self, a self that is continuously pouring itself out, without taking the time to be nourished.

Lacking reflection, we offer to our daily world a preoccupied, cluttered self. In our busyness, we continue to live through a variety of experiences which evoke a host of feelings and responses. When we fail to take time to examine and clarify these experiences, feelings, and responses, they become stored in our inner world somewhat as one stores objects in a spare room until there is time to sort them out. As a result, our inner world becomes increasingly cluttered with unassimilated experiences which may begin to burden and preoccupy us. Not only does our presence to reality become impoverished, but our ability to be open to and to receive continued experience becomes increasingly limited. There is no more space in our cluttered inner room.

Living reflectively is a means of discovering life in and through everyday responsibilities. Life is not what happens after all these obligations have been fulfilled. Rather, life includes whatever unfolds in and through everyday busyness. Life is at the heart of the stuff of everyday responsibilities. It is there that we continue to touch our limits and strengths, to be called forth and stretched beyond ourselves; there that we touch our human brokenness and frailty, and can allow ourselves to be healed; there that our inner dynamism and creative potential are tapped and expressed; there, too, that we experience the gamut of feelings, reactions, and responses.

In the midst of our everyday busyness is hidden the secret of who we are and of who God is calling each of us to become. Living reflectively enables us to uncover the layers of meaning hidden beneath the surface of responsibilities and obligations. As we allow meaning to emerge, we begin to get in touch with our unique way of being in the world. We become aware of what calls us forth and how. Through a reflective presence to reality, we come to see that beneath the countless disjointed events of our day lies the connecting thread of our personal individuality and of our unique approach to life. At that level, we gradually begin to uncover and discover the unique name by which God calls us, a name we are called to live out from the reflective depths of our being.

Furthermore, living reflectively fosters the ability to deal with experience, feelings, and reactions in a natural way, while they are still fresh and alive for us. Thus, our cluttered inner room is gradually put in order, both enabling us to be more totally present to the moment and allowing us to continue to receive new experiences.

Because each of us is limited, our ability to be reflective is also limited. We cannot expect to be reflective about every isolated experience of our day. Vigilantly letting nothing escape us leads only to tension and anxiety, and can be just as devastating as a nonreflective approach to life. As human beings, we are called simply to live through normal everyday life, attempting to remain attuned to daily experience as it unfolds and touches us. Such an attitude demands a sense of presence to persons, events, and situations, as well as a sensitivity to ourselves and to the inner stirrings of our being. It also demands the willingness to dwell with whatever may emerge, however it may speak to us.

Consider the following example. Recently I was driving home from teaching a class. It had been a difficult one in which I had been confronted by a student who was resisting the course. As I drove, I found myself thinking, "This course isn't going anywhere. No matter what I present or how I present it, he just can't tune in. I should have handled that situation differently. I should have been more calm in my approach." On and on churned the self-recriminating thoughts, along with the accompanying feelings of frustration and self-doubt. I felt restless, agitated, upset. My body was tense and tight, and my hands sweaty. I was turning the entire situation in on myself, blaming myself for the student's resistance and for the way I had dealt with him.

As I continued driving, however, I suddenly thought, "Hey, wait a minute. The other students are with me. Their participation and responses indicate that they're getting something out of the course. They were even able to respond to Steve's negative comments. Besides, I'm bringing to this course a genuine expertise. Why should I be so preoccupied with Steve's resistance, to the point of allowing his attitude to determine how I'll approach this class? I'm doing what I can as well as I can. That's all I am able to do.''

As I listened to these thoughts I began to look at the situation somewhat differently. In my agitated anxiety Steve had stood like a giant, as if he were the only one in the class. Now, as these new thoughts emerged, he gradually became one among other students: he had been tailored down to size. I was allowing him to assume his rightful place. My tense body began to relax. My inner restlessness and agitation gave way to some degree of calm. I could begin to breathe freely once again.

This example points to two fundamental ways in which we reflect upon our experience. The tense and anxious preoccupation characteristic of my initial reaction points to an analytical problem-solving approach to life situations, which Adrian van Kaam refers to as introspective reflection. The relaxed distance which led me to look more realistically at the situation points to an awareness of the mystery-aspect of life situations, referred to as transcendent reflection.[1] Let us take a closer look at these fundamental forms of reflection.

Introspective reflection

Introspective reflection is rooted in our calculating controlling self. It is an analytical kind of reflection by which we isolate ourselves or some aspect of a situation from our total reality. Steve, for example, was a resistant student. In my attempt to control the classroom situation, I sought some way to reach him. "Perhaps I should have been more understanding," I thought. "My directness only made him more defensive and resistant." I needed to look at the problematic aspects of what had happened in order to be better able to deal with Steve during the next class. For the sake of the other students, I could not allow him to continue disrupting the class. I was faced with the difficult task of deciding what I had to do in this situation.

Analytical reflection is essentially oriented toward problem solving. This approach is important and necessary in dealing with everyday functional problems: the problem area is isolated, studied, and eventually solved. In treating the personal aspects of our lives, however, we touch upon mystery; we are involved in elements and realities often beyond our awareness and control. To approach life primarily from a calculating, problem-solving stance is to narrow, limit, and attempt to control the mystery that is life. By becoming excessively preoccupied with Steve's disruptive behavior, I unwittingly sought a way to control him. I feared a repetition of what had happened that day. I focused on "solving the problem." In so doing, I lost sight of the fact that Steve was more than his disruptive behavior. I could see no further than his "problem side." Yes, I did have to deal with the "problem." However, I also needed to keep the problem in proper perspective: Steve's disruptive behavior was only part of the mystery of his total person.

The functional culture in which we live unwittingly leads us to become excessively caught up in introspective reflection. We seek to discover every "why" or "how" related to a problem. We become tense, anxious, vigilant. We watch every step and move, lest we become caught in the problem again: I, for example, feared what Steve would continue to do throughout the rest of the semester. I was afraid that he would continue to dominate the class by his resistance. In my anxiety I feared not knowing what to do. Such tension and anxiety could lead me to react aggressively or to approach teaching rigidly, in the spirit of "Come what may, the class must go on." Categorical pronouncements characterized by the inflexible "always," "should," "ought," and "must" indicate that we are allowing ourselves to be controlled by introspective reflection.

Introspective preoccupation is often our spontaneous reaction to conflict, hurt, or misunderstanding. In such painful situations, good relations have been disrupted, becoming difficult or almost impossible to maintain.

Harry Guntrip, an English psychoanalyst,[2] claims that when we are in conflict, we may unconsciously withdraw these unresolved relations into our inner world, isolating their unfulfilled aspects from the totality of the situation in which they occurred. My excessive preoccupation with Steve's disruptive resistance exemplifies this mechanism. These unsatisfying relations do not go away; they become the core of vigilant and anxious analytical preoccupation. We may, for example, begin to analyze insignificant aspects of a relationship, which now take on magnified proportions and become so many contributing factors to the disruption. Obsessed by the need to understand what has happened, we act like a helpless animal trapped in a cage, going over the same incidents time and again. Our mind is absorbed in what happened or did not happen; what was or was not said; how it was said; what we should have done. There may be some truth to our conclusions. However, because all that emerges is filtered through hurt, anger, and hostility, and nourished by analytical preoccupation, the possible kernel of truth becomes lost beneath our anxious, narrow interpretation of the situaion. We no longer see it in its totality but simply focus on how the other has hurt us. More likely than not, we end up feeling like the helpless victim! In my own introspective preoccupation, Steve loomed like a giant. I felt shaken up, insecure, and fearful.

Because of the scientific, analytical culture in which we live, each of us, to some extent, engages in introspective reflection. Our analytical tendencies compel us at times to want to "make things right." In so doing, we may cut ourselves off from the whole of a situation, seeing and judging from the narrow myopic perspective of our limited resources. We make ourselves the center of the world, anxiously avoiding anything that might intrude upon our neat categories, plans, or solutions. Our perception becomes ultimate. Gradually, introspective reflection may unconsciously become a way of life.

All of us, for example, occasionally pity ourselves, feeling upset and depressed because something does not go our way. Immersed in self-pity, we begin to focus on and nourish a host of other situations in which we feel mistreated. We end up feeling like martyrs, selflessly dedicated to an "ungrateful family," or to "students who don't care," or to "people who take me for granted." We become victims of the harsh reality of life.

We all have days when certain aspects of everyday life do seem harsh and difficult to live with. On such days, self-pity may be our natural response; we feel misunderstood, as though we are carrying the world on our shoulders. To experience such feelings is part of being human. We need to own and accept them as ours. However, not being in touch with our natural rhythms may lead us to overindulge in self-pity, thus creating and nourishing our own analytical world in which the main character becomes a tense and anxious "poor me."

Furthermore, all of us at one time or another find ourselves absorbed in the "if only" world, created as a reaction to relational or professional problems. Our "if only" world usually reflects the ideal situation, in which the problem person or circumstance has magically disappeared or has been speedily resolved. This time "successful me" stars in our fantasies, sailing through life smoothly with all obstacles removed. A project is successfully completed because there are no snags. Relationships are easy because there is no "problem person." As satisfying as our "if only" fantasy world may seem, there is little room for growth, for there is no challenge. Consistently nourishing such a world can isolate us from the everyday struggles of problem solving, decision making, or working through relationships. Although all of us at some time need the relief of the "if only," to dwell there can easily become an anxious escape from facing some difficult aspect of our everyday life.

We may also be familiar with the strong, controlling side of ourselves that must push its views through at any cost. We can become so preoccupied with a project or with some personal agenda that the world around us recedes into the background. I once knew someone who frequently became so engrossed in her own world of projects and plans that she was oblivious to those around her. Occasionally during a dinner conversation, for example, she would suddenly say something that seemed irrelevant to what was being discussed. Despite my puzzlement, I tried in my own way to be present to her. I began to understand what was happening one day when she said, "When there's something on my mind, I just cannot be attentive to what's going on." Keeping her introspective world alive demanded so much effort and energy that she had little left to be present to life around her.

When our plans and projects become our ultimate preoccupation, we lose touch with external reality to some degree. We have all known such moments and periods. At these times, we need to reevaluate the nature of our commitments. Can they be rooted *in* reality if they tend to pull us *out* of reality? Or are we so anxiously preoccupied with seeing them through that our world narrows to their size?

Finally, all of us at one time or another experience the problem of being overly conscious of ourselves in a situation. At such moments we anxiously wonder, "How am I coming across?" "What are people thinking?" "Am I turning people off?" "How can I please them?" Such reflections suggest tension and vigilance. We cannot allow ourselves to be or to receive what others may offer us. Rather, we become preoccupied with trying to meet what we perceive as the expectations of others, which in reality may be our own expectations.

Self-consciousness can be our natural reaction to a new situation or to meeting a new person or group of people. As we begin to feel at home with these new additions to our life, we may move beyond our self-consciousness, more able to be simply who we are. However, unless we are aware of the dynamics of excessive self-consciousness in our own lives, this spontaneous form of introspective reflection gradually becomes a habitual way of being for us. Then our life is fraught with undue tension and anxiety. We turn in upon ourselves. We ruminate. We fear losing control of a situation.

As we consider our response to such everyday situations, it is clear that introspective reflection is common to all our lives. To some extent, we all naturally isolate some aspect of our lives from the whole of our reality. Although such isolation is often a necessary and helpful step toward greater self-integration, it must be kept in proper perspective. It would be helpful to be attentive to those aspects of our lives in which we are rigid or feel overly tense, anxious, or frustrated. A gentle, nonjudgmental presence to these problem areas can help us to move to a more balanced perspective, more fully rooted in life.

Introspection and Christian living

Introspective tendencies in our everyday life can be transferred to our approach to our spiritual life. Introspective reflection isolates us from the sacred dimension of life and, ultimately, from God.[3] As we become increasingly engrossed in introspective preoccupation, we are blinded to the sacredness of persons, situations, projects, or plans. Steve had become somewhat of an object for me, one I sought to control. Had I remained introspectively preoccupied with the situation, I would have found it impossible to relate to him as a unique individual. He would have been reduced to "the one who resists"; "the one who disrupts"; "the one who confronts." In such situations, it becomes extremely difficult to respectfully and reverently let someone be. We become calculating, analytical, and controlling. We lose sight of life's mystery.

Moreover, we may begin to see ourselves as isolated from any deeper reality than ourselves. Since our willful self seems ultimate, we come to believe that we must "make it on our own." God is there, somewhere, but distant, uninvolved in our personal lives. We begin to see ourselves as simply thrown into existence by an uncaring, unconcerned God. We are bogged down by our human limitations or by some negative aspect of our background and upbringing. We see ourselves as the helpless victims of circumstances, simply tolerating ourselves and going through the motions of a meaningless existence.

Perhaps the most devastating aspect of introspective reflection is the repression of our innate pre-presence to the sacred dimension of life and to God.[4] We see no farther than our own advantage, our own advancement, our own will, our own projects, our own solutions. Yet, if someone were to hint that we are closed to the reality of God, we would probably react violently in disbelief. After all, we worship and pray. We read Scripture and occasionally think of God. Nevertheless, we may well be closed to the presence and will of God in our personal life.

As we slowly begin to listen to our experience, we may become aware of the many subtle ways that we close ourselves in introspective isolation to the sacredness of everyday life and to God. Under the guise of openness to God's will, for example, we may ask another's opinion, while being more or less consciously convinced that their perceptions will not change our mind. We call that "being decisive." We may compel ourselves to carry on our daily work when we have been ordered to slow down because of ill health. That is "devotion to duty." We may force ourselves through a human-service training program, aware that such a career is against our natural temperament. Rather than listen to our inner self, we struggle on, in the name of "service to humanity." We may refuse to show any kind of reaction to the loss of a loved one. That is "being strong." We may undertake a strict fast for a lengthy period of time while carrying on a full-time job, thereby jeopardizing our health. That is "alleviating world hunger." We may refuse to acknowledge and develop our intellectual ability. That is "humility." In these and many other everyday situations, a lofty ideal can become a cover-up for our own introspective willfulness. When this happens, we are failing to listen to and respect the reality of who we are. Both our limits and our possibilities invite us to stop, look at, and listen to our uniqueness. They invite us to grow in respect and reverence toward ourselves, to realize the sacredness of our personal giftedness. Introspective willfulness, by contrast, focuses on the attainment of some abstract virtue or ideal, in isolation from our personal uniqueness. Respect and reverence, then, give way to willfulness and dominance. Whenever we realize we are forcing things on ourselves in this way, chances are we are making ourselves the ultimate in our life. There is no room for listening to the mystery of God's will for us, as expressed through the reality of who we are. We claim to have it together—our way.

In his overwhelming love, God has gifted us with unique abilities and limitations. Failure to listen to the uniqueness of our being, of our life, of our situation widens the gap between ourselves and God. Because the very nature of our being is a being-at-one-with-God, the result of our introspective control is anxiety, tension, alienation, and aloneness. We stand apart from the sacredness of our personal uniqueness and from God present there.

Legalistic, empty religious observance is a further manifestation of an introspective, ego-controlling approach to God.[5] Our primary concern becomes living the rules rather than a holy life. Since fidelity to the external do's and don'ts of religion becomes all important, we have little room in our life for mystery and ambiguity. On the contrary, we develop a safe and powerful way of living: our way is the right way. Religion, then, is reduced to a willful activity of observing external rules and regulations. We think, plan, and decide our religious life. Consequently, we avoid or deny experiences of God because they do not fit into our isolated introspective system.

Rules, standards, and laws are valuable and necessary. However, they are fundamentally for life, and not the reverse. These vital structures make sense only when they are rooted in and reflect life experience. As such, they do not tell us precisely what we must do. They merely shed light and point the way. For the rigid, legalistic person rules and laws are not only guides and pointers; they become the last word regarding one's spiritual life. Such individuals blindly submit to established external rules and remain spiritually childish. Consequently, their religious observance is divorced from their personal life experience.

When this happens, our relationship with God is reduced to observance of the commandments and the laws of the Church; empty reception of the sacraments; going through the motions of attending mass and of reciting morning and night prayers; a legalistic "loving our neighbor"—and so on. We believe that by doing these things we will satisfy God and we can be at peace. He remains "up there" in heaven, or "out there" in church or chapel, and we remain "here," involved in our own life. God is miles apart from us, watching and judging.

Caught in empty observance, we fail to realize that our relationship with God is more than a willful doing of things. We are blind to the reality that the heart of religion is a spiritual relationship with God. We must do certain things, yes, but more important, we need to remain open to the presence of God hidden in the depths of our being (see Col. 3:3). Jesus tells us that we must be born of water and the Spirit (John 3:1-21); that is, open our human spirit to his Spirit present within us. We must allow his Spirit to permeate our life, our attitudes, our behavior. Thus, Jesus offers us a challenge that touches us more deeply than mere external observance. He challenges us to bring our entire being under the transforming influence and power of his Spirit. For the person caught in a relationship dictated by legalistic do's and don'ts, such a challenge is unthinkable!

The problem of empty religious observance is not peculiar to our own historical period. Throughout his public life Jesus condemned the Pharisees precisely for their hollow observance of the Law for its own sake. They prided themselves on faithful observance, while judging and condemning others for infidelity. Despite Jesus' harsh words, the Pharisees remained obstinate and blind to the true meaning of their relationship with God.

The empty religion of the Pharisees is well illustrated in the parable of the Pharisee and the tax collector (Luke 18:9-15). Both men, Jesus says, came to pray; that is, they came to encounter God, to open themselves to his Spirit and his will. And yet, how different is each man's meeting with the almighty and infinite God! The Pharisee stands erect in self-righteous pride, encountering not God but his own introspective world of pride and contempt for others: "I give you thanks, O God, that I am not like the rest of men—grasping, crooked, adulterous—or even like this tax collector. I fast twice a week, I pay tithes on all I possess" (Luke 18:11-12).[6] In his pride, he is convinced that these things of which he boasts make him perfect. He does not need God. He obeys the Law perfectly, apparently from his own power and ability. What more can God ask of him? He is the seemingly perfect religious person. Yet his boasting betrays an empty heart. He is grateful not to God but to his own ability to look good. Furthermore, he takes pride in believing that he is not like other people. In other words, he fails to recognize his rightful place even before God. His refusal to identify himself with others seems to imply an almost godlike attitude on his part. He stands in righteous self-isolation before God.

The tax collector, by contrast, recognizes his place before God. He acknowledges his sinful creatureliness before the greatness of the infinite God, and lowers his eyes in awareness of his dependence upon his Creator. His attitudes as well as his words convey that his is a real encounter with God, based on a lived awareness of who he is in relation to the Almighty. "All he did was beat his breast and say, 'O God, be merciful to me, a sinner'" (Luke 18:13). In these simple words from the depths of his heart, a humble creature meets his Creator. And "this man went home from the temple justified" (Luke 18:14).

Jesus spoke this parable not only to the Pharisees and the tax collectors of his day; he speaks it to us today, for there is in each of us something of both the Pharisee and the tax collector. At times, we stand apart from God by our insistence on mere external observance for its own sake. We may not be so openly self-righteous as the Pharisee, but we can live through the motions of prayer and worship. Perhaps we judge and condemn others who do not live as we do. Or again, we may refuse to accept continued change in the Church or in religious life. In a word, we become closed to any way but our own. We grow rigid and inflexible. External observance becomes a safe wall erected between God and us.

Much more risky is the option to be like the tax collector, for openness to God means willingness to accept that he truly is our Creator, that we are dependent upon him. Openness to God means consenting to emerge from behind our wall of legalistic defenses by questioning the personal meaning of a relationship with God. At first this thought may seem frightening and threatening to our need for security and certainty. However, in openness to God, our fear can give way with his grace to a spiritual surrender and peace. In our openness, we—like the tax collector—can accept our place before God: that of poor, weak, and limited creatures. The Almighty, then, takes us to himself. In him our sinfulness is healed. Through him we are made whole.

At the heart of introspective reflection is the self-in-isolation, cut off from some dimension of life and, ultimately, from God. Although most of us may not be deeply enmeshed in an introspective way of life, we can probably identify to some extent with the foregoing descriptions of introspective reflection. Introspection is a natural and necessary form of reflection. It enables us to examine a situation in isolation, to see our role in it, our way of being, our attitudes, in order to place it within the broader perspective of our total lives. For example, I may be dealing with or working through anger, either in my journal or with a friend, a counselor, or a therapist. During the working-through process, it may be necessary for me to look at and temporarily stay with my anger. I may have to reflect upon such questions as "What makes me angry?" "How does my anger feel?" "What happens inside me when I feel angry?" "How do I express my anger?" Throughout this process, I may be angry at everything and everyone. A word, an action, a simple glance are enough to call forth my anger. The angry feelings may be so intense and powerful that I become obsessed with having to "let them out." For a time, I may feel as though I have lost control of myself. I am angry with myself, with others, with situations, even with God. As I move through this difficult process, my intense repressed anger slowly dissipates as I write about it, talk about it, express it, and allow myself to feel it. With time and help, my "angry self" will gradually begin to find its rightful place within the context of my whole self. Angry feelings continue to well up, but less intensely. I continue to be aware of them and to learn to deal with them in wholesome, healthy ways. Anger no longer preoccupies or controls me; rather, it becomes a normal expression of my total self. Thus, introspective analysis and working through can be a means of authentic growth. Such periods are temporary, however, and should serve to deepen us—they are not ends in themselves.

Since we are embodied spirits we are capable of another kind of reflection. Our human spirit, which is open to the whole of reality, has the potential to lead us beyond isolated introspective reflection. As helpful as analytical reflection can be at times, it must eventually yield to the deeper call of our spirit if we are to become the persons we are beckoned to be.

Transcendent reflection

Whereas introspective reflection isolates us from some aspect of life through anxious analysis and calculation, transcendent reflection carries us beyond the immediate situation. As humans, we have the ability to move beneath the surface value of persons, events, and things in order to ponder their deeper significance. Consequently, we are not merely floaters on the surface of reality, but deep-sea divers able to discover hidden treasures in its depths. Martin Heidegger describes such reflection as "releasement toward things" and "openness to mystery."[7] In other words, transcendent reflection invites us to release our control over life in order to allow it to be as it is and to unfold in its own way.

When we are open to the mystery of persons, events, situations, and things, we can let go of our desire to control, to isolate in neat categories and slots. We can release our introspective hold on life, thus allowing people and events to emerge and unfold as they are. Such an attitude is risky and can be frightening to our calculating self, whose source of security is in the predictable, the programmed, the planned.

Let us return to Steve. In my introspective preoccupation his disruptive resistance had become a major problem. The situation had to be solved if I were to continue teaching. I began to move out of my introspective stance when I was able to become aware of other aspects of the situation: others too were annoyed by Steve. During the class some of them had had the courage to refute Steve's arguments. I was putting much time and effort into the preparation of each class, and my background was different from Steve's; perhaps we would never see eye to eye.

Each of these insights moved me beyond my isolated introspective stance. I began to place Steve within proper perspective as one among many students. I became aware of his uniqueness. Now, I could try to respect him according to my limited ability.

Although I continued to feel uncomfortable with Steve throughout the remainder of the course, I was able to move beyond my anxious feelings as I continually reminded myself of the positive realities that emerged in transcendent reflection. Moreover, throughout the course, I remained concerned for him as a person, attempted to reach out to him in the limited ways that were possible, and prayed for him.

According to Heidegger, "releasement" is an important aspect of transcendent reflection. Releasement, he says, requires both a "yes" and a "no" attitude toward the things of our world. We say "yes" to these persons, events, and things as being meaningful-for-us. We benefit from the advances of science and technology, for example. We foster healthy and wholesome relationships. We learn to discover meaning in the events of our lives. We affirm and accept the various elements that make up our lives. The attitude of releasement, however, demands that we also say "no" to certain aspects of these realities. We grow from them but we also let them be, refusing to allow them to control our lives. We deny them the right to dominate us. Releasement, then, is an attitude of letting go and of letting be.

The attitude of releasement, for example, enables us to refuse to allow ourselves to be controlled by our hurt and angry feelings. Our "no" to nurturing these hostile feelings is at the same time a "yes" to move toward reconciliation inasmuch as that is possible. Whereas introspective reflection uses persons, situations, events, and things exclusively for its own advantage, transcendent reflection allows them to be as they are and perceives them in proper perspective in relationship to the reality of our whole life.

In the situation with Steve the attitude of releasement enabled me to relax a little. I could not deny that I was upset, that I wanted to do something about the situation. For a time, I did allow these feelings to control me. As a result Steve loomed large before me. In my introspective stance, I allowed him to do precisely what I was fighting against: to control me. The moment of release occurred when I found myself saying, "Hey, wait a minute. . . ." With those words I began to gain distance from the situation. I started to question and to let go of my overwhelming feelings. I regained my perspective, thus placing the disruptive event within the context of the whole situation. Letting go of my feelings allowed me to move.

Disengaging oneself from introspective preoccupation happens ever so slowly and imperceptibly. Working through conflict, misunderstanding, or overwhelming feelings demands time, patience, and delicate care. It also demands courage. Such movement remains possible for each of us, however, because we are embodied spirits. We are capable of eventually gaining distance from analytical preoccupation in order to glimpse the mysterious, uncontrollable aspects of a situation.

Transcendent reflection and Christian living

Openness to the transcendent mystery-aspect of everyday life enables us to get in touch with the deepest ground of all reality: God. Each of us is already present to the sacred dimension of life.[8] This is evident in our respect, reverence, and awe for the world around us. We may stand in spontaneous awe before the beauty of a sunset or of the raging sea, or find ourselves in quiet reverence before an infant. The spontaneity of such responses indicates that awe and reverence are an innate part of who we are, a natural response to mysterious realities that lie beyond our limited powers of understanding. These already existing attitudes need only be uncovered and nourished. More important, though, these attitudes also point to the reality that as humans, our deepest self is hidden in God (see Col. 3:3). The almighty, eternal God is present in the core of our being. He is Spirit of our spirit, Life of our life. He becomes the ultimate reality within which the isolated and disjointed events of our everyday life take on deeper meaning and assume their rightful place within the total context of our lives.

As Christians we are called to grow into an awareness of God's presence in our everyday lives. Such an awareness is rooted in a transcendent approach to life. As we grow in our ability to free ourselves from anxious preoccupations, we learn to see ourselves and various aspects of our lives as rooted in and emerging from the mysterious will of our loving and caring God. Within this transcendent perspective, we begin to see our life and efforts as small contributions toward the ongoing unfolding of humanity. We are no longer strangers and aliens, but citizens with the saints (Eph. 2:19) immersed in the mystery of all creation, at one with those who have lived before us, all who are presently living, struggling, and growing, and those who will follow us. Such a transcendent awareness fosters a relaxed approach to life. Although we must fulfill everyday responsibilities and obligations, the awareness of being but a small part of a mystery far beyond ourselves gives us the freedom to be comfortable with what is possible for us: making our unique but limited contribution to the unfolding mystery of creation in the brief time that is ours.

For the Christian, transcendent reflection is a valuable means of putting things into place. As the mystery of God grows increasingly real for us, our plans, projects, and everyday lives become relative. Our strong need to control gradually gives way to a relaxed presence to reality. While doing what we can to modify and improve our lives, and while working for the success of our projects, we allow them to be, recognizing that they are rooted beyond the immediate here and now. They are important, yes; they are not absolute. In the situation with Steve I slowly came to realize that although I would continue to seek ways of dealing with his disruptive behavior, my primary responsibility lay in doing what I could do professionally within this limited classroom situation. Though I continued to struggle with my feelings, reflective distance enabled me to see that Steve's challenge was part of God's mysterious call to growth.

As a result, I was better able to move with the situation rather than attempt to control it.

The back-and-forth movement between introspective and transcendent reflection is characteristic of our human condition. In developing a transcendent approach to life, it is imperative that we respect and accept the rhythm of our individual pace. Because of the functional, problem-solving culture in which we live, we may remain vulnerable to excessive introspection for a long time. We cannot deny or repress analytical reflection, for it is an intrinsic part of being human. As such it is necessary and helpful. Our challenge as individuals is to create a balance in our lives between introspective and transcendent reflection. Growing toward such a balance is an ongoing process. Perhaps the most we can hope for is the gift of awareness of our excessive tendencies, and the strength to move beyond them according to our limited ability to do so.

Peter, who for three years listened to Jesus, followed him, and walked the dusty roads of Palestine with him, can be a source of comfort as we strive toward a balance in our lives. The impetuous and passionate Peter had become one of Jesus' intimate friends. In faith, he recognized Jesus as Messiah. He stood by Jesus after the discourse on the eucharist when others were questioning, doubting, and abandoning him. "Lord, to whom shall we go? You have the words of eternal life" (John 6:68). He was one of three who witnessed the Transfiguration, who in amazement and enthusiasm had wanted to build tents on Mount Tabor. He had been in the garden during Jesus' agony, heavy with sleep and too tired to be present to Jesus during his time of need. Peter's love for Jesus, however impetuous, was as real as he was and blinded him to his human limitations. Nothing seemed too difficult for him. He would give his life for this Jesus whom he loved. Though everyone else abandoned him, Peter would stand by him. In his passionate love, the apostle was unable to hear Jesus' warning foretelling his denial. Peter was strong, self-sufficient, able to sustain any eventuality. In introspective isolation, he counted on his own strength. His strong, bold, impulsive approach to life had always worked for him. He had no reason to believe that it would fail him now. The rugged fisherman who had weathered countless storms had come to believe that his own resources could see him through any situation.

However, all that changes drastically when Jesus is confronted by the soldiers in the Garden of Olives. Typically impulsive, Peter attempts to save the situation: he draws his sword and severs Malchus's ear. Imagine his dismay and frustration when Jesus heals the man and orders Peter to put his sword away. What is happening makes no sense to Peter; fear and confusion overwhelm him. His bold strength and his love for Jesus fade into the background as he becomes introspectively centered upon himself and his well-being. Later, fearful and bewildered, he vehemently denies even knowing Jesus. The crowing of the cock brings his moment of truth: the moment of recognition that suddenly pulls him out of his introspective self-centeredness. "The Lord turned around and looked at Peter, and Peter remembered the word that the Lord had spoken to him. . . . He went out and wept bitterly" (Luke 22:61-62)—tears of sorrow and repentance, tears that move him beyond his isolated self to focus on the Jesus whom he so deeply loves, to whom he has sworn to remain faithful. In the compassionate look of that moment of truth, when his eyes meet those of Jesus, Peter is pulled out of his bold arrogance into presence to his Lord. Jesus' look of love touches the core of Peter's being. In that moment, his life is transformed. He begins to rely more on the Lord's strength within him than on his own; to trust more in the Lord's words than in his own; to become increasingly receptive and responsive to the Lord's way rather than to his own willful ways. This moment of truth is a moment of conversion and reformation—a moment of deeper rootedness in the Lord, emerging from the humble recognition of his own human weakness and sinfulness. This arrogant, impulsive Peter becomes the humble, more docile Peter, who is able to hear with his heart Jesus' piercing question, "Simon, son of John, do you love me?" (John 21:16). He becomes the sensitive Peter who feels hurt because the question is addressed to him a third time. He becomes the Peter who has deeply surrendered to his Lord, and who can now respond, "Lord, you know everything. You know well that I love you" (John 21:17). The transformed Peter can rest in Jesus' love for him and in his for Jesus.

Peter has touched the depths of his own weakness. In his moment of truth, his love for Jesus is purified and ultimately deepened. He has moved from introspective self-sufficiency to transcendent dependence upon his Lord. His strength and his passionate love for Jesus are no longer rooted in arrogance, but rather in spiritual awareness of his human weakness and frailty.

We know from the Acts of the Apostles that in the midst of the struggles and controversies of the early Church, Peter often reverted to his natural willful ways. However, his personal experience of God's love eventually enabled him to move toward a more transcendent perspective.

For most of us, like Peter, introspection will often be our first reaction to a person or situation. Such a reaction may be temporarily helpful and necessary. Moreover, most of us are emerging from a predominantly introspective spiritual formation in which the focus seemed to be on our own effort, our own prayers, our own discipline, in a word, on our own will. Through prayerful, isolated self-examination, we tried to fit into the mold of some abstract ideal, often overlooking the Lord's unique path for us as concretely expressed in our personal gifts and strengths, limitations and weaknesses. Often, the result was tense and anxious striving for some unattainable ideal as we unconsciously lived from the belief that we by our own efforts could make ourselves holy and pleasing to God.

In recent years our approach to spirituality has gradually become rooted in individual uniqueness and in the Word of God in Scripture. Consequently, the focus of our spiritual growth and development has shifted. We are learning to focus on God. Yes, prayer structures and human efforts remain necessary, but the tense, straining effort of introspection is no longer called for. Rather, we are invited to root ourselves in God, allowing him to shape and fashion us through our personal uniqueness, through his Word, through the liturgy and sacraments, through the concreteness of our everyday lives. In faith-filled reflection, we grow gradually in our ability to see others, ourselves, and our lives as concrete expressions of his will for us. As we grow in this approach, we become increasingly aware that God, rather than our introspective willfulness, is the master of our lives. He presents us with the ongoing challenge of growing receptive and responsive to him.

As we focus on God, he gradually opens our eyes to our ungraced ways, those obstacles to his presence in our lives. Like Peter, we too meet our Lord and face our moment of truth: our human weakness, frailty, and vulnerability. At such times, we may be called to let go of our arrogance, or we may be invited to discipline our unruly anger, jealousy, or hatred. We may be asked to move beyond our pettiness. Listening and responding to God's movement in our lives requires that we too personally address ourselves to Jesus' question to Peter, "Do you love me?" That is, "Do you love me enough to allow me into your life in order to transform you into the graced self I have called you to be? Do you love me enough to let go of your introspective willfulness and to respond to the ongoing challenge of refocusing, readjusting, and redirecting your ways? Do you love me enough to see the beauty with which I have gifted you, to allow me to work in and through the person you are? Do you love me enough to let go of your will in order to allow my will to be accomplished in and through you?"

For most of us, such movement from a willful, introspective approach to spirituality to a transcendent rootedness in God's will for us remains an ongoing challenge. As products of a highly willful culture which extols human control and production, we naturally tend to transfer our willful ways of doing to our spiritual relationship with God. Often it is only after we have exhausted all our human resources that we begin to surrender to God's ways for us. Perhaps the greatest challenge of our spiritual lives is that of allowing our willful ways to be influenced and reformed by a transcendent approach rooted in God's Spirit at the heart of our being.

As embodied spirits, we are continually called to move through and beyond introspection to transcendence in whatever limited way such movement is possible. Thus our reflective moments and eventually our reflective lives are rooted in the deepest truth—that of God's continuously unfolding mystery of love.

---

1. Adrian van Kaam, *In Search of Spiritual Identity* (Denville, N.J.: Dimension Books, 1975), pp. 172-196. Throughout this chapter the terms "introspection" and "transcendent reflection" are used according to van Kaam's understanding and description: "Introspective reflection implies a focusing process in which the background is either blurred or lost. Both inwardly and outwardly, it is divided. It purposely loses sight of the totality and goes at its object aggressively. . . . Transcendent reflection is the opposite of introspective. In it, we may reflect upon ourselves, others and nature to become one with a Divine Source, mysteriously united in an Eternal Origin" (pp. 174-175). "Each kind of reflective presence to ourselves—introspective or transcendent—has its own purpose, time, and place. Our vision of ourselves as interwoven with the whole of reality should be primary, the introspective view secondary" (p. 177).

2. See Harry Guntrip, *Schizoid Phenomena, Object Relations and the Self* (New York: International Universities Press, 1969), pp. 19-23.

3. See van Kaam, *Spiritual Identity,* pp. 172-196.

4. See Adrian van Kaam, *Personality Fulfillment in the Spiritual Life* (Denville, N.J.: Dimension Books, 1966). In this book, van Kaam

develops the theory that the human person is implicit pre-presence to the whole and Holy; that is, as embodied spirit the person is present from birth to the transcendent dimension of life and reality.

5. See William Kraft, *The Search for the Holy* (Philadelphia: Westminster Press, 1971), pp. 162-165.

6. All Scripture quotations and references throughout this book are from *The New American Bible.*

7. See Martin Heidegger, *Discourse on Thinking,* trans. John M. Anderson and E. Hans Freund (New York: Harper Torchbooks, 1969), pp. 11-57.

8. Van Kaam, *Personality Fulfillment,* pp. 13-44.

Chapter two

Embeddedness in the everyday

Among the time-honored traditions of my family is our annual Christmas Eve family reunion. For the past nineteen years, the ritual has remained essentially the same. Children, spouses, and grandchildren joyfully gather at "Mémère and Pépère's" house. Throughout the evening, the crèche is pointed out to the younger family members and the Christmas story is simply and naturally passed on from parent to child. Santa appears on the scene with gifts and surprises for all. Dad has polished his baby-grand piano for the occasion, and all sing the timeless melodies of Christmas carols. Punch, soda, and homemade goodies are enjoyed by all as we relax together and catch up on what has been happening in one another's lives. A spirit of joy, lightheartedness, and closeness permeates the evening. Over the years, as my younger brothers and sisters, nieces and nephews have grown, the evening has been prolonged, and various families have lingered, savoring how good it feels to be together. The time for good-byes inevitably creeps up on us, and with the regretful au revoir is the hope that next Christmas Eve will once again bring all of us together.

During this past year's celebration I was particularly struck by the implicit educative process of this tradition, for three nieces and nephews under two years of age were present. For five-month-old Rhianna, this year's family gathering was a first. She was content to be nursed, held, and cuddled. Nineteen-month-old Adam was aware of the many people around him, and this year Santa was okay—at a distance. Little Adam was intrigued by Pépère's piano playing, and became excited when he discovered that he too could make music by striking the notes on the higher end of the keyboard. This year Adam also discovered the homemade holiday goodies, and limiting him proved to be a challenge for his parents. For twenty-three-month-old Kendra, this Christmas was most exciting. Her eyes, as well as her entire little body, expressed freshness and excited wonder as she stood looking up expectantly at Santa. Her natural spontaneity spoke to all of us of the beautiful simplicity and innocence of a child totally absorbed in the immediacy of the moment: carefree and able to let herself be open to life. Not yet exhibiting the possessiveness characteristic of children, she accepted Santa's gifts only to hand them to someone else. What she received mattered little to her. Her primary focus was Santa.

As young as these children were, they were being exposed to and, at the same time, unconsciously assimilating a whole tradition. For each of them, this fun-filled evening, like so many other daily routines, was a learning experience. In a very natural way, each of them was being taught that "This is part of what belonging to this family means."

We, like them, are born into a world that existed before us, into a family and society long independent of us. Like baby Rhianna, or little Adam or Kendra, each of us has grown into the preestablished ways of our family and society. Unconsciously, we have absorbed the values, attitudes, beliefs, perceptions, and ways of being and doing characteristic of our family. With time, each of us has learned the concrete meaning of belonging to our particular family. We have also absorbed the ways of our society: our American life-style; our success-oriented culture; our production-minded mentality; our democratic form of government; the political structures of our city, town, state, and nation. We have absorbed both the strengths and the weaknesses of our family and culture: their open-mindedness as well as their prejudices; their respect for others as well as their injustices.

The impact of unconscious cultural absorption and assimilation came home to me forcefully several years ago when I participated in an international congress held in France; delegates came from France, Austria, Canada, and the United States. Living in France for those few weeks was an eye opener for me. The simplicity of life there impressed me, and I found myself getting along rather easily without the many gadgets and commodities that were indispensable back home. In traveling through the countryside I saw people well on in years busily working in their gardens. Their closeness to the earth as well as their personal war experiences seemed to have given them unusual strength and vigor. By the same token, I was intimidated by the natural forthrightness of the French. I was astonished by their lack of practicality on the everyday level, and inspired by their love for the arts.

Working with people from various countries and cultures also made me keenly aware of my American ways. I remember well a frustrating work session during which an international group of us had to put together a working outline based on the day's general session. My American mentality led me to want to get the task done simply and directly by working from main ideas and themes. The French participants seemed more at ease with a long, wordy, complex outline, while the Austrians brought a keen sensitivity to language and expression to the discussion. The Canadians patronized the Americans and failed to understand our perspective. My immediate reaction to being part of this group was confusion and frustration. To me, the direction seemed clear. My American way was the best. Why couldn't the others see that? What could have been accomplished in a short time dragged on endlessly. Why did we need to engage in so much discussion? After all, this was a working draft, intended merely to express ideas that had surfaced during the general session. It would have to be worked and reworked, discussed and rediscussed before anything could be finalized. Why all this fuss?

Although I left this meeting feeling frustrated, I gradually came to terms with our cultural differences. As the congress unfolded, I grew more open to other ways and views. I left enriched by this cultural experience and more keenly aware of my embeddedness in my American ways.

Each of us grows in the unconsciously absorbed worlds of our family and society without, for the most part, questioning their existence. Generally we do not challenge our family values, nor do we wonder why we do what we do. We also submit to societal codes and traditions without questioning their reason for being. As Americans we would not think of greeting another person with a profound bow rather than with the familiar handshake of our culture, nor would we drive on the left side of the street. We take our world and society for granted, as part of our common everyday experience. Maurice Natanson refers to this taken-for-granted belief in the world as the ordinary attitude.[1]

We bring this attitude to many areas of our lives, to our daily routine as well as to relationships with other people. In the ordinary attitude we go through the motions of daily life, more or less aware of what we are doing. Only when a new or different element is introduced into our routine way of being or doing do we become more conscious of our world and our behavior. When our electricity fails we suddenly appreciate the ease with which we normally flip the switch. Or when the city bus-drivers decide to strike, we are suddenly confronted with having to find another way to get to school or work. In both situations, our taken-for-granted world has been disrupted. We feel uncomfortable and uneasy, for our familiar resources are no longer adequate.

The same is true of relationships with other persons, especially those we associate with each day. Often we respond to what we expect to see rather than to what is actually there. For example, we may look at someone we know intimately and have been with over a number of years without seeing the real person. We have come to take that person for granted, making the individual a victim of our ordinary unreflective attitude. Often it takes a sudden change in that person's appearance to make us take a second look and see the person as he or she really is. Such things as a drastic change in hair style, a loss of weight, an injured arm or leg, or a strong difference of opinion may awaken us to take a closer look at the other person. Again, the glance of a third person who sees our friend from another perspective may suddenly shatter our old, habitual image.

The ordinary attitude, then, is an integral part of our being in the world. It is part of our pact with the world; in a sense, it anchors us there, providing stability and security.

Advantages of embeddedness

If we are to function comfortably and effectively in our everyday world, we need to experience stability and security in life. We need to feel at home, to have a certain place and space, and to be able to accept ordinary routine things as they are without constantly questioning their why. Imagine the useless expense of energy if we had to worry about whether or not the light will go on when we flip the switch; or whether the car will start when we turn the ignition; or whether or not we will receive our salary at the end of the week, or find food at the supermarket when we do our grocery shopping. Rather, we take these things for granted, simply expecting them to be there.

In a sense each of us moves sleepily through life. We live with the belief that our familiar ways of being and doing will continue to see us through. Or we realize that we have moved through life rather comfortably and successfully with our values and principles; why should we question them? Again, we may believe that our way of thinking is the right way; why then should we even consider the possibility that another's insight might be helpful? Without our realizing it, our embeddedness in the ordinary attitude becomes a comfortable, secure way to make some sense out of the chaos of the world. Implicitly, the ordinary attitude, to some extent, defines our limits and possibilities and sets the perimeter of our lives. Within this space we can remain relatively secure in the face of life's countless uncontrollable insecurities. Consequently, when some aspect of our taken-for-granted world is disrupted, we often become tense, anxious, and frustrated.

I recall a city bus-drivers' strike that occurred during my graduate-school days. In the house of studies where I lived we relied on public bus transportation to travel to and from school. Our dependence on the buses encouraged us to dismiss rumors of a possible strike; in our minds it could never happen. The basic trust of our ordinary attitude was soon shattered, however, when the strike became a reality on a Friday night. Even then, the power of the familiar convinced us that by Monday all would be well again—after all, the drivers were obligated to thousands of workers and students who rode the buses each day. So we thought! Days dragged on as each morning and evening we listened for news of the end of the strike. In the meantime, some of us organized a car pool; others grouped to take a taxi. In either case, there was the give and take of accommodating various schedules and obligations. One student's remark captures well the general feeling of uneasiness: "I never realized how much we take bus transportation for granted. Ever since this strike, I use so much energy each day just trying to figure out how and when I'm going to get to and from school—it's exhausting!"

Our basic at-homeness had been shattered. Suddenly we were awakened to having to find other alternatives for getting to school. Only then did we realize the power and necessity of our confident embeddedness in the world. To expend such energy on ordinary everyday activities diminished our effectiveness in the more important aspects of daily work and responsibilities. Embeddedness in the ordinary attitude, then, is an important energy saver for all of us. It is the secure place from which we can move out to risk exploring new horizons, the familiar to which we can comfortably return.

Furthermore, embeddedness can also foster a reflective attitude. Without some kind of basic trust and rootedness in life and in the world, we become tense, anxious, and overly vigilant. We become so absorbed in simply getting through each day that daily experience passes us by. We have neither time nor energy to listen to our life or to allow meaning to emerge; our inner world becomes cluttered with preoccupation and worry about relatively simple issues. As a result, we feel disoriented and unable to reflect on the multifaceted dimensions of life as it presents itself to us each day. Rather than resting in the gift of life and allowing it to reveal itself in quiet reflection, we fret, worry, and fear.

Some time ago, for example, I moved to a new state to begin work in a new area of the ministry of spirituality. Having previously spent a week at this center, I had met the staff; I had experienced the nature of the ministry; I had become familiar with the house and with the immediate vicinity. Although I eagerly looked forward to this new challenge, I felt uprooted from all that had been familiar to me. I had to form new relationships. I had to adjust to new ways of thinking and being. I had to adapt to a new and varied schedule. I had to learn where things were in the house, and I needed directions to get anywhere. I had to adjust to new facets of ministry. Every person I met was a new face and a new name. Although I was very happy in my new situation, I often longed for something or someone familiar during those first months. I longed to be with and talk to people I knew, those with whom I had a shared history. Occasional trips back to the familiar territory of my home state were always welcomed. There, I felt I could breathe and simply be.

The reflective dimension of my life was significantly affected by all this newness. Adjusting to countless new dimensions of everyday life minimized my reflective presence to reality. I was preoccupied with trying to find my place in so much newness. Consequently, I came to my journal and to prayer feeling scattered and disoriented. My mind raced in a hundred directions. Being present to myself and to God in prayer and quiet reflection seemed impossible. Agitation and preoccupation now inhabited my relatively quiet inner space. Such simple, nonreflective activities as putting things away, getting to the next town, and calling someone by the right name, all became important energy consumers that hindered my ability to reflect and to be present to experience.

With time I grew into greater familiarity and ease with the many aspects of my new situation. The ordinary everyday activities that initially required so much energy gradually became familiar, thus demanding less conscious attention. Simultaneously, my inner self was freed, enabling me to be increasingly present to reality and to rediscover my inner quiet. As a result, I was once again able to be reflectively present to my everyday experience and to God in prayer.

Each of us in our own way has to make sense of our lives and our world. In order to deal with the many disruptive factors that enter into our experience, we possess an innate tolerance for disruption. However, when certain life situations stretch us beyond our own particular level of tolerance, we become almost totally absorbed in the mere process of coping. Everything else seems to fade into the background. Consequently, our reflective attitude as well as our reflective presence to reality is also temporarily diminished. Our survival instinct compels us to give priority to whatever threatens our stability and security. As a result we can develop our reflective life only when we experience a certain basic security, for without this necessary groundedness, we are agitated, disoriented, scattered. Embeddedness, then, is the anchor that frees us to be reflectively present to the richness of our everyday experience.

Disadvantages of embeddedness

As necessary and helpful as the ordinary may be, it does present certain dangers. Although our natural trust in life and in the world can foster a reflective attitude, it can also make us unreflective. We become set in the values, principles, traditions, and ways of being and thinking that we have unconsciously absorbed through our lives. We see no reason to question, evaluate, or change. Our natural security, then, can gradually become rigidity. Comfortableness with our ways can evolve into settling into a routine existence, and, without realizing it, we slip into a superficial way of life. In some respects, we become the hollow men and women of whom T. S. Eliot wrote.

He described these hollow individuals as having no mind of their own. They have spent their lives absorbing popular values and principles, merely going through the motions of living. They are stuffed—embedded in a way of life they have never questioned. Such men and women have never personally responded to the challenge of life. Rather, they have allowed themselves to be tossed to and fro by the waves of every passing fad, of every extolled value and principle. They are basically good people who have unknowingly and indiscriminately absorbed most everything around them. As a result they are stuffed, yet hollow. Their inner life has been paralyzed. Their gestures remain lifeless and meaningless.

Because of our unconscious embeddedness in life, each of us is, to some extent, hollow and stuffed. Most of us have probably become complacent in certain aspects of our lives. Perhaps we are caught up in a life of willful control and achievement, which leaves little or no room to question the deeper values of life. As a result our reflective life is considerably diminished because it is not nurtured. We become so totally absorbed in the immediate, or in achievement, or in action that we live a surface existence. We either abide rigidly by unquestioned values or tend to live our lives according to the values of significant others or of the crowd. Consequently we are not centered within ourselves and tend to move through life sluggishly and sleepily with very little personal reflection on our experience.

Embeddedness and the life of the spirit

Embeddedness in our familiar world also affects the life of our spirit. Our spirit constantly calls us to move beyond ourselves, to become who we are not yet,[2] in such simple ways as the inner call to become more patient, understanding, or firm. At other times the inner restlessness of our spirit invites us to take stock of our lives. For all of us, such moments can be painfully disturbing and we may seek to remain safely embedded where we are. Consequently, the power of embeddedness may lead us to repress the haunting call of our restless spirit. Someone once shared with me that he could see clearly what God was asking of him and where he had to move in his life, but, he added, "I just don't want to listen. It's too difficult and I don't have the courage to do what I have to do. I know that someday God will put me in a corner and I won't have any choice, but right now, I just don't want to move. I need to stay where I feel safe and secure." As I listened to him, I had no doubt that he was consciously choosing to silence the voice of his spirit in order to remain in his safe little world. He was well aware that paying attention to his spirit demanded a strength and courage he did not have at that moment.

Most of us can probably identify with this resistant attitude. The power of embeddedness easily convinces us that we are better off where we are, that moving beyond ourselves is too difficult and challenging. And so, for the time being at least, we repress the restlessness of our spirit. Its voice is increasingly dulled, and its life is stunted.

Along with fostering an unreflective way of life and the dulling of our spirit, our embeddedness in the ordinary attitude can also endanger our personal uniqueness. The power of embeddedness leads us to absorb values and convictions that have been imposed upon us by family, educators, society, or any other significant person, group, or institution. It is possible that in our sleepy embeddedness, we grow into adulthood with a child's concept of honesty, love, and self-expression, with a child's understanding of religion, or with prejudices toward persons of another race, color, creed, or class. By failing to question these values, we insulate ourselves from further personal growth and development, safely hidden behind such unquestioned absolutes as "always" or "never." Our unique self remains dwarfed.

Part of becoming an adult implies the willingness to examine and modify what we have learned as children, to make it our own, tailored to our unique individuality. Throughout our lives we all experience the tension between the desire to remain in our comfortable, secure world and the call to move beyond what we have been taught in order to personalize and integrate it into our adult lives. For most of us, personalization is a process we would not undertake on our own. Often it is forced upon us through the natural disruptions of everyday life.

Awakening through disruption

The process of personalizing usually happens when our ordinary attitude is disrupted. An insight, a confrontation, sickness, failure, birth, death, an unexpected event, the entrance of a new person into our lives, a local, national, or international event—each of these life situations creates some degree of inner uneasiness or restlessness. Such events pull us out of our embeddedness, throw us back upon ourselves, and call us to reflect upon what is happening. In quiet reflection we can make our own some truth, value, or principle that we have previously taken for granted.

My sixteen-year-old nephew Mark, for example, was present at the Christmas Eve family reunion. From the beginning of his life he has participated in this family tradition, and over the years it has become part of his value system. He arrived at this past year's celebration earlier than the others and sat pensively in a rocking chair, watching my mother, sisters, and me scurrying about the kitchen with last-minute preparations. We were aware of his presence but too busy to pay much attention to him. Suddenly he said, "Why is it that this Christmas Eve celebration is so different for me now? I still look forward to coming and I still enjoy this get-together, but I don't feel the same way about it as I did when I was a kid. I used to get really excited, and now I don't. It's like there must be something wrong because I don't feel the same way." My mother tried to explain to him that what he was experiencing was all part of growing up; that as we mature, Christmas takes on other meanings and calls forth different feelings; that those feelings are all right, even though they are not the excited, bubbly emotion of a small child. I added that often the commercialized atmosphere in shopping malls and in television commercials presents an image of how we should feel at holiday time. We are told that we ought to be joyful, excited, enthusiastic. When we do not feel that way we may begin to believe that there is something wrong with us. Mark listened attentively to all of this and agreed with what we were saying. It made sense to him, but he seemed to need time to think about it.

In his own adolescent way, Mark was facing a moment of awakening. Through the strange and new feelings he was experiencing, a significant taken-for-granted aspect of his life had suddenly been disrupted and was being called into question. The reflective process had already begun, even as he faced his own feelings and began to articulate what he was experiencing. He could have chosen to repress and deny his feelings, thus continuing to live in sleepy embeddedness. His decision to face and express his experience was his way of beginning to look at a tradition he had previously taken for granted.

As Mark reflects on his experience he is also beginning to personalize this family tradition. In his own way he will make it his own, gradually allowing its personal meaning for him to emerge. He is choosing it for himself in his unique way rather than having it chosen for him by his parents or the rest of the family. Chances are that next Christmas Eve he will be present more from personal choice than from routine.

A certain anguish accompanies any disruptive moment of awakening, similar to that experienced by a lost child. Despite the consoling words of strangers trying to help and the encouragement that "everything will be just fine," the child remains frightened and inconsolable in an unfamiliar environment. So it is as we face any disruption in our lives. We feel we have been uprooted. The familiar disappears, and our at-homeness is shattered. For a time we are alone, lost, and confused.

As a result of this experience, however, we come home to a new level of awareness. Everything in the ordinary attitude is retained, no longer in the sleepy state of embeddedness but rather as a personalized, reflected-upon reality. The world has not changed; rather, through reflection our experience of it has been transformed. We are more aware of living consciously through experience and more open to discovering its unique meaning for us.

Disruptive situations are part of every human life. As we remain open to the unfolding of life, we periodically find ourselves confronted by strange and unexplainable situations. We can do nothing to force these situations to happen; they simply occur, initiated from outside and beyond ourselves. Regardless of whether or not we want to accept them, they are there. Of course, such situations are far more disruptive when they touch us personally. Each day, for example, I pick up the newspaper and read about birth and death, love, joy, and suffering. At times, I can feel something of the joy or sorrow that the persons involved are experiencing. Nevertheless, I remain detached from their actual situation, looking in from the outside.

My response is very different, though, when I myself must confront a disruptive situation, such as the bus drivers' strike. Suddenly my familiar patterns and responses are useless. I am confused and, in a sense, lost because the familiar no longer works. I begin to question the reason for the event, the disruption, the inadequacy of my familiar ways. Through no choice of my own, an uncontrollable event has caused a break in my familiar way of living. This break is a moment of awakening which invites me to reflection and personalization.

It is important to note that not only extraordinary events disrupt our embeddedness in the familiar. The simple joys and sufferings strewn along life's journey may also have that effect, as can our own feelings and reactions to a situation. It matters little whether this disruption is extraordinary or subtle. What is important is that we remain open and attentive to it in whatever form it presents itself, for within it lies the invitation to continued growth.

Despite the disruptive force of sickness or failure, or of our feelings, each of us is free either to listen to its personal meaning for us or to shut it off entirely and remain securely embedded in our little world. The decision to accept or to repress the disruptive situation is ours. For each of us, there are times when we may be unable to face or deal with disruption. At such times our freedom of choice is limited by the need to hold our seemingly fragile lives together. As a result, we may unwittingly retreat into the security of the familiar. When this happens, we close our eyes and ears to the possibility of further awakening. At such moments, we become more deeply entrenched in an unreflective, sluggish way of life. At such times it is helpful to remember that we are not alone. In our fear and weakness, the support of a close friend, a family member, a spiritual director, or a counselor or therapist can enable us to face, move through, and grow from the pain of disruption.

Disruption in any form is painful and difficult, for it forces us to grow into greater awareness. In the face of such situations, it is important that we understand and respect our possibilities and limitations, as well as our tolerance level, so as to facilitate moving gently and gradually through the process of awakening to a deeper level of reflective living. Because of the power of embeddedness, this process is never finished. Rather, it is ongoing, presenting us with the continuing challenge of a richer life.

Embeddedness and Christian living

Embeddedness also affects our relationship with God. Just as we absorbed familial and cultural values, so too, at a very early age, we began unconsciously to assimilate the religious values and traditions of our parents. Thus, we may have grown up saying daily morning and night prayer as a family, attending mass and receiving communion on Sunday, going to confession regularly, learning our catechism, and being taught the meaning of sacrifice, particularly during the Advent and Lenten seasons. We were also taught to share, to be kind and honest. We learned a whole set of values. We may have heard bible stories which left an impression upon us. Implied in this learning process was the message, ''This is what being a Catholic is all about.'' And so we grew into adulthood, feeling safe and secure in the religious ways and values that had been handed down to us. We knew what we had to do in order to be a ''good Catholic,'' and for the most part we did not question our relationship with God. We became embedded in a routine Christian way of life.

Saint Teresa of Avila describes the "good Christian" as being in the third dwelling-place of her interior castle:

> I believe that through the goodness of God there are many of these souls in the world. They long not to offend His Majesty, even guarding themselves against venial sins; they are fond of doing penance and setting aside periods for recollection; they spend their time well, practicing works of charity toward their neighbors; and are very balanced in their use of speech and dress and in the governing of their households—those who have them. Certainly, this is a state to be desired.[3]

Teresa goes on to describe these persons as living well-ordered, balanced lives in every respect. They have reached a level of exterior perfection. She cautions, however, that the danger at this level is that such persons become complacent about their spiritual lives and settle into this dwelling-place without moving to a deeper intimacy with God. Consequently, she says, it is possible to spend one's entire life at this level. The security enjoyed here engenders a very real fear of risk which persons must work through in order to deepen their relationship with God.

At this stage, we are somewhat like the rich man of the Gospel (Matt. 19:16-22) who came to Jesus with an open heart wanting to know what he had to do in order to gain eternal life. To Jesus' response that he keep the commandments, the man replies that he has done this since his youth. The commandments are familiar to him; he has lived them. However, his question, "What must I do?" suggests a certain inner dissatisfaction and reveals that he may now be open to looking at these familiar commandments in a new light. For him, this could be the moment of personalization, the moment of being called out of his complacent way of "keeping" the commandments. He seeks more. When faced with the one thing further that he must do, however, he is saddened. He cannot risk giving up and living without his many possessions. He cannot face the insecurity of the unknown to which he is being challenged. Consequently he goes away sad, settling for a complacent life with his many possessions.

The same danger exists for each of us, unless we personalize the spiritual ways, values, and attitudes we have absorbed over the years. This personalization process is painful and challenging, precisely because it disrupts the security of our old and familiar ways.

The Second Vatican Council clearly has had a profound effect on the life of the Church and on our individual lives. To a greater or lesser degree, each of us has been shaken out of our complacent religious beliefs and practices. Almost overnight, we experienced changes in the liturgy. As a Church, we began to dialogue with other Christian denominations. The focus of religious education moved from a question-and-answer to a scriptural approach. Parish councils and committees came into being. Orders and congregations entered into the process of renewal, which affected every aspect of life from exterior habit, rules, and structures to members' inner relationship with God. More recently we have witnessed the birth of various lay movements and lay ministry programs.

Though we may have welcomed the renewal of the Council, we have also experienced some degree of tension and anxiety in regard to certain changes, for our security was ruthlessly disrupted, and we had no place to rest our feet, so to speak. As a result, many of us became resistant and defensive, reactions with which we may still be dealing. Such reactions are natural, for we were asked to die to some of the ways and attitudes that had become sacred to us. However, through this disruption, we were being invited, perhaps for the first time, to reflect upon our relationship with God, to begin to make our own what we had previously taken for granted. Even today, almost twenty years after the Council, the challenge of personalizing spiritual values and attitudes remains.

Throughout recent years it has become evident that the Church will never return to the changelessness of pre-Vatican times. Consequently we must accept ongoing evaluation and adaptation, within the context of a certain necessary stability, as part of our Christian life. Occasionally, I hear lay Christians declare, "I'll be glad when they finish with all these changes!" and religious remark, "I so look forward to getting our final constitutions." Such statements imply the legitimate need in all of us for stability and a healthy embeddedness in life. However, we need to guard against the possibility of embeddedness unwittingly leading to entrenchment. One of the most challenging ascetical practices of our time may be the discipline of trying to remain open and responsive to God's ways as manifested through ongoing change, adaptation, and renewal in the Church, in religious communities, and in our own lives. Developing spiritual openness and flexibility is no small matter in the face of the powerful inner pull toward complacent routine. As members of a pilgrim Church, we are invited to engage actively in the pilgrimage, to be on the move, following a Lord who had no place to lay his head.

A sister who has been in religious life for a number of years recently shared with me her own struggle in this area. Even after the renewal of Vatican II, she had continued to maintain essentially the same prayer structures that had served her well for many years. Now, however, she was beginning to feel uncomfortable with them. She felt confined and frustrated by one hour of daily personal prayer, a set time for spiritual reading, and another set period for reflection on her day. Her prayer life seemed compartmentalized, yet she was extremely reluctant to adopt any other way. These structures had worked well for her, and she had grown through them. Now she feared that changing them would make her permissive, lax, and undisciplined. Overcoming her apprehension, she tried setting aside a day a week for prolonged prayer, reading, and reflection, a structure that emerged from her own need and seemed more compatible with the intense demands of her ministry. She felt comfortable and at peace with this arrangement, and reported that this prolonged time seemed to nourish her relationship with God throughout the days that followed. This new structure seemed right for her at this specific period in her life. For a long time she had struggled with letting go of her former way, primarily because for so many years she had been taught it was the "right" way. The breakthrough moment of awakening came one day when she found herself saying, "Who decided that one way is the right way for everyone? What makes it so right?" At that moment she realized that she had to discover and be faithful to what seemed right for her at this time. Letting go of the familiar structures of many years was indeed risky, but the power of this awareness gave her the strength and freedom to step out of the embedded ways she had outgrown, in order to respond in fidelity to where God appeared to be leading her.

Whether the personalization process is related to the structure of our prayer life or to a Scripture passage, to the Eucharistic liturgy or to reception of a sacrament, to a reading or a homily, it immerses us in the mystery of dying to some aspect of our taken-for-granted ways in order to enter into a fuller life in Christ. In a very real way, our entire life is a call to walk with Jesus into the Paschal Mystery of passion, death, and resurrection. From the first moments of existence, we are forced out of the security of the womb into the huge, cold world. The developmental process ensures that we grow out of the cozy warmth of mother's arms and onto the floor to begin exploring the world around us. In the same way, we move from the security of crawling on our hands and knees to the insecurity of walking, with the many risks of falling or of being knocked down. Gradually we move from the safety of family and home to begin exploring the neighborhood, and then into the unknown world of school, per-haps the greatest trauma of these early years. So, the process continues throughout life as we are confronted by the various life crises that are part of being human. At each stage we live through an exodus: a being called out of the secure and familiar, a dying to some aspect of our taken-for-granted world, only to be led into the insecurity of the new and unfamiliar and, finally, to new life.

The Samaritan woman offers us a vivid example of the dynamics of moving out of embeddedness into a fuller spiritual life (John 4:4-42). On this particular day, she comes to the well to draw water, to perform an ordinary everyday chore. In the process she is suddenly jolted out of her cultural embeddedness by a Jew who asks her for a drink. According to tradition, Jews had nothing to do with Samaritans. Furthermore, a Samaritan woman was regarded as ritually impure; Jews, therefore, were forbidden to drink from any vessel she had handled. She re-sponds to this request with a certain defiant arrogance: "You are a Jew. How can you ask me, a Samaritan and a woman, for a drink?" She is by no means a docile, compliant person! This man's request makes no sense to her, and she tells him so.

Undaunted by her resistance, Jesus responds on a spiritual level, calling her to move beyond the immediacy of her daily task and beyond the culture shock she is experiencing in the presence of this Jew. He speaks of "God's gift" and of "living water." The woman, however, remains on the level of the literal and the obvious. She challenges Jesus, saying, "You don't even have a bucket. Where do you expect to get this water that you speak of?" In her own way, she seems to be telling Jesus that he does not know what he is talking about.

Uncomfortable and ill at ease with what Jesus has to say, she is no longer on the solid ground of her customary world. Not only has a cultural barrier been broken; this man is saying things that make no sense to her. Since she cannot grasp his spiritual message, she interprets him literally, trying to salvage something of the solid and familiar.

Jesus once again engages her, provoking her and calling her to further reflection. He speaks of life-giving water that will become a fountain and provide eternal life. The woman once again hears Jesus from the security of her familiar world. She desperately wants this water—not for eternal life, but simply to satisfy her own needs: this water of which Jesus speaks will quench her thirst, and save her the daily trip to this well. In her own way she is saying, "Yes, please, give me this water. It will make my life easier." Her desire for the water Jesus has to offer—although it is literal and motivated out of a practical concern—indicates an initial openness to him. Until now she has strongly resisted both his presence and his words. At this moment, her resistance is weakening. Her cry for this water speaks of her own thirst, not only for physical water but also, unknowingly, for the living waters Jesus offers her.

Jesus, aware of her movement toward openness, now leaves the topic of "water" and "thirst" and challenges her on another level. By asking her to call her husband, he forces her to face her own messy and confused life. At this point, the woman is thrown back upon herself. Her immediate defensive reaction is to deny that she even has a husband. She is backed into a corner, most probably feeling frightened and uncomfortable. She has been pulled out of her familiar world and is left with no resources on which to rely. She has no alternative but to begin looking at her life, perhaps for the first time. This moment of truth becomes a moment of recognition as well: she sees Jesus as prophet and Messiah. In the joy of having been deeply touched, she leaves her water jar, symbol of her complacent embeddedness, and runs off into town to proclaim that she has found the Messiah.

The story of the Samaritan woman is ours as well: a story of being invited to move beyond ourselves in some ordinary, everyday aspect of our lives, as God comes to us through another person, or a simple event or situation; a story of defensiveness and resistance, of seeking refuge in our familiar ways, attitudes, and values; a story of being backed into a corner and of having no choice for growth except that of opening ourselves to God and to his movement in our lives. It is a story, finally, of coming to a deeper recognition of who God is for us, of discovering new and deeper life that ultimately becomes our witness to the reality of God in our lives.

Despite her defensiveness and resistance, the Samaritan woman allowed herself to be called forth from her embeddedness in order to meet Jesus and let him come into her life. As baptized Christians, we commit ourselves to enter over and over throughout our lives the mystery of Jesus' passion, death, and resurrection. Just as Jesus came into the life of the Samaritan woman through an ordinary activity, so too does he enter into our everyday lives, inviting us to move one step beyond where we are. What he asks of us may range from the relatively easy to the extremely difficult. Whatever his demand, our personal faith in him leads us to believe that he walks with us through the darkness in order to lead us into his light. He presents us with the challenge of response: am I willing to risk moving out of my complacency in order to follow him into the unknown? However minimal our openness, he enters in only to bring to greater clarity his image within us.

---

1. References to Natanson's theory throughout this chapter are from Maurice Natanson, *The Journeying Self: A Study in Philosophy and Social Role* (Reading, Mass.: Addison Wesley, 1970), pp. 8-17.
2. For a further development of the dynamics of the emerging self, see van Kaam, *Spiritual Identity.*
3. Teresa of Avila, *The Collected Works of Teresa of Avila,* vol. 2, trans. Otilio Rodriguez and Kieran Kavanaugh (Washington, D.C.: Institute of Carmelite Studies Publications, 1980), p. 306.

Chapter three

The rhythm of presence and distance: heart of a reflective attitude

There is an appointed time for everything,
and a time for every affair under the heavens.
A time to be born, and a time to die;
a time to plant, and a time to uproot the plant.
A time to kill, and a time to heal;
a time to tear down, and a time to build.
A time to weep, and a time to laugh;
a time to mourn, and a time to dance.
A time to scatter stones, and a time to gather them;
a time to embrace, and a time to be far from embraces.
A time to seek, and a time to lose;
a time to keep, and a time to cast away.
A time to rend, and a time to sew;
a time to be silent, and a time to speak.
A time to love, and a time to hate;
a time of war, and a time of peace.

(Eccles. 3:1-8)

This familiar passage from the Book of Ecclesiastes reminds us that our lives are made up of the ebb and flow of varied rhythms. Implied in these verses is a sense of movement and dynamism. Our lives are not static; rather, they are filled with various experiences that continually call forth from us as many varied responses. In their simplicity and directness, these verses reflect the significant rhythms that weave their way through our lives.

Besides the significant moments described in this passage, many ordinary taken-for-granted rhythms fill our everyday lives. Each day, we find ourselves routinely living through the rhythms of getting up and going to bed; of working and relaxing; of laughing and crying; of being with other people and being alone; of being awake and asleep, and so on throughout our day. These natural movements not only put some necessary structure into our days but they are also important for our well-being and continued development as persons.

Another such rhythm is that of presence and distance. Countless times throughout each day we are called forth to be attentive to various persons, places, events, and things. At times, the demands of being attentively present may enrich and fill us. At other times, they leave us feeling scattered or drained. At such moments, we need to step aside, to catch our breath, so to speak, in order to allow the experience of presence to settle within us. We need distance.

As we consider growing in a reflective approach to daily life, the rhythm of presence and distance emerges as the heart of this reflective attitude. In developing our ability to be present to everyday experience and to allow ourselves to dwell upon that experience in quiet distance, we become increasingly reflective about our lives. Whether or not we are aware of it, the rhythm of presence and distance is a natural movement for each of us. We need only recall the many times we find ourselves thinking or feeling such things as "I need to get away"; "I need space"; "I need to be with people"; "I'm tired"; or the times we find ourselves watching the clock, anticipating the next coffee break, the end of the workday or a specific activity. Such moments make us aware that the rhythm of presence and distance is already present within us. The intensity of presence leads to relaxed distance.

Despite this fact, respecting our personal rhythm remains an ascetical challenge for most of us. As we have seen, our ability to be present to the various aspects of our everyday life is diminished by our embeddedness. The fullness and richness of life are veiled by our expectations, or we mechanically go through the motions of our activities in a sleepy way. Our ability to be open to receive the gift of the moment is thus limited. Since we cannot be fully present to the persons, events, and situations of our day, neither can we fully distance ourselves in order to discover meaning and depth. We live somewhere in between, in the never-never land between presence and distance, simply floating through life.

Our natural rhythm may be further affected by our culture's demand that we produce, achieve, and succeed. Many of us feel inwardly driven by the need to do things and to keep pushing. There is always something else to do, another project or another meeting. We run from one area of involvement to another, feeling tired and tense. Our ability to be present to whatever involves us is then diminished. Since we are caught in a seemingly endless cycle of activity, there is little possibility of gaining distance from ourselves or our involvement. We are compulsively driven by the need to keep going. Consequently, our reflective life becomes impoverished.

Because of the power of embeddedness and our immersion in the cultural drive to do and to produce, getting in touch with our personal rhythm of presence and distance requires effort. For a long time we may need to consciously attempt to bring an awakened presence to life; we may find ourselves needing to listen to the body signals of fatigue, discomfort, and tension in order to begin respecting our need to slow down and step aside. Or we may need to make conscious efforts to quiet our racing minds, already involved in tonight's activities or tomorrow's agenda. Whatever our area of personal asceticism, it is important that we be gentle and respectful of our unique pace, for only in gentleness can we hear the faint voice of reflective meaning, insight, and awareness. We may be tempted to *make* ourselves receptive and reflective. We need to remember, however, that we are considering a spiritual attitude—a way of being for our spirit—which cannot be forced. Attitudinal change and growth occur slowly and imperceptibly. The asceticism of our personal effort remains vitally essential, but it must be tempered by gentleness, reverence, and a respectful willingness to stay and move with emerging awareness.

Presence

The word "presence" is defined as "the act of being in a certain place and not elsewhere." This definition touches the heart of presence. It challenges us to be fully where we are, or with whatever we are involved in. It invites us not only to be physically present to our world but to bring a total inner presence as well: to be in a certain place and *not elsewhere*. All of us can recall those frequent moments in our lives when we have been physically present but mentally, emotionally, or spiritually absent to a specific life experience. We may listen to another person, for example, while being inwardly preoccupied with formulating an answer. Or we listen to a speaker, and at some point find ourselves miles away from what is being said. Sometimes our presence to another person is colored by inner preoccupation with resistance or hostility toward that individual. We may be so absorbed in our agenda of things to do that while washing the dishes or the car we are already planning another project. In such situations we are in a certain place *and elsewhere* as well. Unwittingly, we are sucked away into the future or we become entangled in the web of our own feelings and preoccupations, while the freshness of the present moment slips through our fingers. As a result, we close ourselves to the gift of the moment, which we neither see nor hear because of our lack of presence.

Being totally present in a certain place and not elsewhere remains a challenge for all of us. More often than not, our attention is scattered. However, there are times when we may be inwardly free enough to allow experiences of presence to happen. Such moments are gifts, reminders that we can ready ourselves for moments of total presence. With time and patience we can develop a genuine ability to be present to whatever enters into our daily lives.

One day I was walking through a familiar section of town. It was a crisp and breezy spring day. The bright sunshine was a welcome relief from the damp weather of the previous days. As I walked along I gradually let go of my preoccupations, simply enjoying the sunshine and the crisp air. I felt invigorated and stimulated. Suddenly, I became present to the street on which I was walking. I had walked along this street hundreds of times without ever really noticing it. For the first time it was becoming real for me. I found myself paying attention to my steps, looking at the surface of the pavement and thinking of those responsible for producing the macadam, as well as those who had paved it many years before I ever walked on it. I reflected on those who had planned the street, those who had mapped out the direction it would take, those who had determined its length and width. I also found myself thinking of the construction workers whose heavy labor of many days and weeks had leveled the soil and whose work had enabled the mapped plans to become a reality. Here I was, walking along the street, planned and constructed by people I never knew and who never knew me, a street over which countless automobiles drove each day. As all of this spontaneously came to me, I found myself experiencing a sense of respect and reverence for the street. I respected it for what it was and revered it for its enabling role in the lives of so many. It carried life and facilitated life for those who used it. I also felt appreciative to those unknown persons whose talent and work had created it. As I walked, I felt united with all whose lives touched the same road. I felt my own insignificance.

I had obliviously walked this quiet side-street hundreds of times before. It was a street like any other, yet on this day it had come alive for me. Suddenly it was not only a paved road but also a street with a life and history of its own—a street that had been there long before me and that would continue to exist long after me. It had become my link to men, women, and children of the past, present, and future. During my walk this day, I had become spontaneously present in a way I had never before known. My total self was there, present to the street and its history. I was quiet enough to let it speak to me of itself. I was able to listen to its story.

I have often walked this street since this experience. Occasionally the sense of presence has returned. However, for the most part, that experience is only a memory—a sacred one which has developed into a sense of respect and reverence for this and other roads on which I travel.

A closer look at this ordinary experience enables us to become aware of some of the qualities essential for developing an attitude of presence: a degree of inner freedom; the ability to become engaged in the experience; and a certain vulnerability.[1]

Inner freedom is basic to developing a sense of presence to life. As we have already seen, inner clutter on any level minimizes our presence to life situations as well as our ability to be called forth by them. I had very often walked the street preoccupied; feelings and experiences consumed my energy and minimized my presence to what was around me. The street was simply there for me to traverse while I continued to be inwardly busy. On this particular day, however, I had let go of some of my preoccupations. My inner world was quiet enough to enable me to take in what I was experiencing. Because I was relatively free, I could be open to the moment. For the first time in my life I was able to listen to the story of this long-familiar street.

Such moments of openness simply happen. Neither programmed nor forced, they come freely as gifts. However, it is important that we ready ourselves for such moments. Often we fail to be present to the world about us simply because we do not take time to be attentive to the seemingly insignificant aspects of daily life. For example, have we ever let ourselves feel the refreshing warmth of the water running over our hands as we wash them? Do we sometimes take the time to really taste the food we eat or the tea we drink? Do we ever stop to watch a toddler discover and explore the world around her, or take the time to listen to an adolescent or an elderly man? Can we allow ourselves to be present to the plants we water or the clothes we wash? How often do we stop to watch the snow fall or to listen to the sound of the rain? Our lives are made up of activities that beckon us to stop, look at, and listen to them, to discover the richness that lies beneath their surface.

Antoine de Saint Exupéry opens us to the mystery of life in *The Little Prince*. In his parting words to the little prince, the fox shares with him the secret of life:

> "It is only with the heart that one can see rightly; what is essential is invisible to the eye."
>
> "What is essential is invisible to the eye," the little prince repeated, so that he would be sure to remember.
>
> "It is the time you have wasted for your rose that makes your rose so important."
>
> "It is the time I have wasted for my rose—" said the little prince, so that he would be sure to remember."[2]

The fox invites the little prince and us as well to become attentive to life with the eyes of our hearts. He suggests we take the time to look beneath the obvious and to discover life's hidden beauty. Only with the eyes of the heart can we begin to see the invisible beneath the visible and the mystery beneath the factual; it is only with the heart that we can touch the essence of life and allow ourselves to be touched by it. The eyes of the heart invite us to slow down and to respect even what seems—at first glance—insignificant. Whatever we are experiencing begins to come alive for us as did the familiar street on which I walked. It took on a life of its own and began telling me its story, one that could be heard and listened to only with the heart. As a result, this familiar street became sacred to me because I had been allowed to penetrate the invisible and to become immersed in mystery. The same can be true of any life experience to which we are willing to bring a heart-filled presence.

The fox also reminds the little prince that wasting time is important. Initially, such advice may seem foolish to those of us who are caught up in the hectic pace of everyday living. However, as we allow ourselves to move beyond such rationalizations, we may gradually see that wasting time is an integral part of being present. Simply being with another person is a waste of time if we are looking at life from a merely functional perspective. The same is true of attending a concert, watching a sunset, taking a walk, or standing in line. Nothing is accomplished. Yet in the experience of wasting this kind of time—of being present to life—we gradually discover that we have been enriched far beyond the functional level. Wasting time with another may blossom into friendship. Attending a concert may inspire us. The setting sun may awaken and enliven our spirits. Taking a walk may refresh us or help us to regain a lost perspective. Standing in line may be the opportunity for a reflective pause and foster a sense of presence to those around us. Such moments can be enriching. In the process of wasting time, life may become precious, as did the little prince's rose.

Finally, taking the time to be present to experience also has a healing effect. Occasionally we feel alone and cut off from people and distanced from life. Such feelings are painful; when engulfed by them we wonder if things will ever be right again. This last encounter between the fox and the little prince bears some similarity to such times. Both of them experience the sadness of separation. It is interesting to note that the little prince repeats the fox's words in order to *remember* them—to allow himself to be *re-membered* and healed. In our times of aloneness, presence to the moment can enable us also to be re-membered, that is, to experience a renewed sense of belonging to a world greater than ourselves and our concerns. Presence to the moment we call "now" leads us to awareness of the mystery of our oneness with all of life. Such a moment can have a healing effect upon us and lead us to regain a lost perspective or to see the relativity of a situation that had perhaps become absolute and all-absorbing.

This attitude of inner freedom and openness to the moment differs significantly from our everyday need to control, manipulate, and solve life's problems. Our everyday conscious self is usually uncomfortable with openness and mystery. Remaining open to the unpredictability of mystery is difficult. It is true that on the everyday practical level, we must necessarily bring many things to closure: decisions have to be made and tasks accomplished. Despite these demands, however, it remains possible to allow our practical decisions to be influenced by a sense of respectful presence. A few years ago, for example, an urban developer bought a school building in a small town. It had been empty for a number of years and had fallen into disrepair. Because many of the townspeople had been educated in that school, there was much sentimental value attached to it. The developer's plan was to transform this building into apartments for senior citizens. Initially he intended to alter the facade. However, he finally decided that although it needed repair, he would keep it essentially the same. His practical decision emerged from a sense of respect for the history of this edifice in the town. Today it is an apartment building for the elderly, standing as a tribute to a developer whose sensitive presence to the townspeople and to the structure led him to preserve a bit of local history.

Such decisions are not always possible. However, it is important in our decision-making processes, significant or not, to attempt—as much as possible—to approach life with a sense of inner freedom. Therein lies the challenge of presence.

Such spiritual readiness prepares us to become actively engaged in whatever we are experiencing. Each of us brings to any life experience the baggage of our personal history, perception, and unique approach to life. We have the power to place upon any experience the stamp of our unique interpretations. Because no two persons see things exactly the same way, each of us possesses the power to touch and influence others and to make a difference in their lives. We have all known the effects of our moods on others or the effects of our affirmation or non-affirmation of another. Depending on the nature of our relationship, the effects of our power can range from minimal to highly significant.

This power of presence which emerges from an attitude of respectful openness is not a controlling one. Rather, it is a gift that we bring to the other, a power that calls forth, enables, and touches the other.

Such power is clearly evident in the life of Jesus. Wherever he went he was surrounded by crowds. The power of his presence touched and called forth the best in people, drastically transforming the lives of those who encountered him. We read of the conversions of Levi, the tax collector; of the woman taken in adultery; of Zacchaeus; of the Samaritan woman. We read of the search of Nicodemus. We read of the many whose sins were forgiven and whose physical and spiritual health was restored. Jesus himself was aware of his power and his ability to touch others. In the story of the woman with a hemorrhage, we are told that Jesus "was conscious at once that healing power had gone out from him" (Mark 5:30). But his response to Pilate, "You would have no power over me whatever unless it were given you from above" (John 19:11), suggests that Jesus was also very much aware that his power came from his Father.

Jesus' example speaks clearly to us. Our unique power of presence can influence and touch another to the degree that we remain aware that whatever power we have is God's gift to us. Through his power in us, we grow in our ability to be present to others. We touch their lives. We engage the other. God's power in us is a respectful power in service of life.

The final aspect of presence is our willingness to be vulnerable. Our attitude of respectful openness leads us to realize that the power of presence is not limited to ourselves. Others are also endowed with power that calls us forth. We need only reflect upon our reaction to others to realize how their presence influences us. At times we feel comfortable with one person and uncomfortable with another. We are open to one and closed to another. With one we can be ourselves and with another we put on a mask. Just as each of us has the ability to call forth the other, so the other possesses that same power in regard to us.

Respectful presence to life experience invites us to be vulnerable enough to risk becoming engaged in life and to permit ourselves to be touched and changed by our experience. We allow the other to penetrate our defenses. We let go of our controlling tendencies or our strong emotions to become present to an experience on its own terms. On the everyday level, such respectful vulnerability urges us to be called forth by the majesty of the thundering surf, allowing it to reveal to us our own insignificance. Or we are moved by the beauty of a concert that touches the depths of our sensitivity. We may share time with a close friend, allowing him or her to tap our deepest potential. Or we are called forth by a news broadcast describing a nation's struggle for justice, allowing it to release our compassion for suffering people and our rage toward oppressive systems. On the day of my experience with the street, I had become vulnerable enough to listen to its story. As a result, I became experientially aware of my own insignificance in light of the total history of this street. I was touched by the experience.

In this and countless other situations, our vulnerability places us in the position of learner: some aspect of our embedded self is awakened; our consciousness is raised; we become aware. In some way, our presence to a person, event, or thing transmits an attitude that says, "I come to you with an open mind and heart, willing to be with you, to walk with you, to learn from you, to allow myself to be influenced and touched by you."

Again we find ourselves having to let go of our desire to control the encounter. We need to relinquish our expectations in order to be open to the unfolding moment and to allow the situation to emerge in its own way. We may also need to work through our initial resistance in order to be influenced by and to learn from the experience. Being vulnerable is risky and, at times, frightening, for we do not know where the experience of presence may lead. However, if we avoid the vulnerability that openness requires, we remain encased in our masks and unable to be fully present to life.

The people of Nazareth, as portrayed in the gospel, offer a stark contrast to the vulnerable Jesus, who could allow himself to be influenced by the many people, events, and circumstances that entered into his life each day. He was touched by suffering, sickness, and death. The lilies of the field, a grazing flock of sheep, a returning fishing boat, and a poor widow called him forth as so many opportunities to speak of spiritual truths. His own townspeople, however, held to their stereotyped image of the Messiah. They could not allow themselves to step out in vulnerable presence to this man whose reputation had spread throughout the neighboring villages. They could not risk letting go of their beliefs and expectations. After all, he was simply "one of them"; the Messiah would be someone special. There was nothing extraordinary about this carpenter's son. Rather than trying to be open to the mystery of the person of Jesus, they preferred a controlling approach. They wanted immediate answers and so they raised functional questions: "Where did he get all this? What kind of wisdom is he endowed with? How is it that such miraculous deeds are accomplished by his hands? Is this not the carpenter, the son of Mary, a brother of James, Joses, Judas, and Simon? Are not his sisters our neighbors here?'' Their final reaction to Jesus seems to touch the essence of minds closed to the mystery of his person: ''They found him too much for them'' (Mark 6:2-3). As a result, they could not be touched by Jesus because they were unable to be present to him as he was.

As we gently discipline ourselves to be present to our experience, scattered moments of presence gradually grow into an attitude of presence. We become mindful; that is, we develop the ability to be present to our unfolding life experience in an ongoing way.[3]

To live consistently present to reality is a difficult challenge. Our everyday busyness, preoccupations, and obligations hold us captive. Our work and responsibilities often involve projecting and planning for the future: next week, next month, six months from now. A friend involved in pastoral ministry says that she often finds herself absorbed in planning the parish celebration of the next liturgical season or programs for the next group of students. She dislikes the fact that by the time the liturgical seasons of Advent or Lent, Christmas or Easter arrive, she has already lived through them. Many of us find ourselves dealing with similar situations. We are called to live in the present moment, yet our responsibilities demand that we be future-oriented. At such times we are challenged to be present to our planning, which is the immediate task at hand. Simultaneously we are called to allow ourselves, according to our limited ability, to remain in touch with other aspects of life around and within us.

We may at times find ourselves thinking, ''If only I could get this done, then I could take time to be present to my experience.'' Such compartmentalized thinking closes our eyes to the giftedness of our everyday responsibilities. These are not obligations to be fulfilled before we can be relaxedly present to more peaceful activities. Rather, daily obligations are the stuff of our everyday lives to which we are called to be present in the way that is possible for us at the time. Mindfulness is the simple awareness of whatever we are involved in at the moment. In such an awareness, we get in touch with deeper levels of meaning beyond the everyday functional dimension. Gradually, the many compartments into which we fit our various everyday obligations break down. We no longer only work, shop, clean house, prepare meals, do laundry, watch television, drink coffee, relax, or walk. Rather, these various activities are bound together by the delicate thread of a gentle presence. They are all part of daily life and, as such, part of our life at this particular time on this particular day. Such an attitude frees us from being drawn into the future by the next thing that has to be done. In relaxed presence, we bring life to and, at the same time, discover life in our varied daily activities and obligations.

For a long while I regarded such activities as cleaning, cooking, and doing laundry as tasks I had to do. I felt that these chores took me away from more important things such as preparing a conference, reading, praying, or writing. I squeezed them into time slots and more or less did them on the run. I somehow managed to do all the things I had to do, but with significant body tension and inner restlessness and agitation. I often found myself preparing a meal engrossed in something I had read or planning how I would make up for this lost time.

One day while I was peeling vegetables I realized, "this is part of my daily life. This task is part of what I'm called to do, just as vital as other so-called more important things. It's not a waste of time." That awareness changed my perception and pace. My usual style was to rush around the kitchen feeling tense and agitated, aiming only to get things done. Now, I found myself spontaneously slowing down and being present to the action of peeling the vegetables, respectfully setting the table, at each place mindful of the person who would be seated there. I moved around the kitchen more slowly and deliberately as I became increasingly present to the meal I was preparing. Since that day, preparing meals has become for me a more reflective experience.

No longer a waste of time, it has become "my time," like many more important activities.

How do we begin to gather our scattered minds in order to become mindful? One effective way is to become aware of the rhythm of our breathing. When we find ourselves feeling dispersed, unable to be present to the moment, or when we find our minds wandering into the past or the future, we can gradually regain a calm, mindful presence simply by watching our breath: being aware of the rhythm of inhaling and exhaling; of breathing in a long breath or a short one.[4] Such a discipline changes our focus. As we concentrate on our breathing, we begin to let go of whatever pulled us away from the present moment. Our mind is slowly freed. Our inner self once again is calmed and quieted.

Because we are so often scattered, the discipline of presence is precisely that: a discipline. The ability to become aware of the rhythm of our breathing is within reach of all of us. However, because breathing demands no thought or reflection, we do not pay attention to it. Raising it to the level of awareness requires conscious attention, a practice that may strike us as simplistic and inadequate. Nevertheless, it is an effective time-tested method, used through the centuries by numerous individuals, both Christian and non-Christian, from the East and West.

We must remember, however, that the technique is merely a means intended to enable us to develop an attitude of presence. At the beginning we may find ourselves preoccupied with it. Gradually, though, it will settle into its rightful place—a means.

Moreover, we may discover that other rhythmic patterns in our everyday lives have the same effect. The rhythmic noise of a machine, the regular ticking of a clock, the rhythm of the surf washing the beach, the steady sound of our footsteps—any of these can enable us to refocus and thereby regain our sense of presence to life.

Growing in an attitude of presence to the moment, we come to realize that nothing in daily life is unimportant or insignificant. Rather, every person, place, situation, thing, or activity is precious and laden with mystery and meaning. Each one invites us to slow down, to be present, and to listen to its story as it reveals to us something of its hidden meaning.

Distance

In developing a reflective attitude, the moment of distance is no less important than the moment of presence. The word "distance" is derived from the Latin *distare,* meaning to stand apart or to be separate. The moment of distance, therefore, can be described as that moment when we step back from the experience of presence to an external reality in order to become present to our inner selves. In that self-presence, we stop, look at, and listen to the experience to which we were present; we separate ourselves from it so as to learn from it. In the stepping aside we gain objectivity. We look at various aspects of the situation as they emerge in quiet reflection, examine our feelings, and let them settle within us. We gradually begin to place the experience in proper perspective within the context of our lives.

Recently I sat down to work on this book for a period of time that promised to to be quiet and uninterrupted. Shortly after I began to work, the doorbell rang. It was an unexpected visitor involved in a photography project, asking me to participate. I tried to become present to her. However, knowing that these short hours were my only free ones that day, I felt annoyed as precious moments slipped away. I could feel my body becoming tense, and realized that I would never accomplish what I had planned to do. Eventually, we completed the project and I returned to writing. A short while later I was again disturbed by a repair man, and then by a telephone call. Needless to say, my body tension and inner annoyance resurfaced. This was not the morning I had planned! After the phone call I found myself spontaneously standing back from these interruptions and from my annoyance. In that natural stepping-aside moment, I gained sufficient distance from my own frustration as well as from these various disturbances to acknowledge how I felt and why. I was able to allow the experience to speak: no, this was not the way I had planned the morning, but this was the reality. My body tension and annoyance told me that for the time being I was not free enough to write: any added interruption would simply increase my frustration. As I listened to these feelings, I realized it was not the time to work on the book. Thus, I found myself moving from writing to house cleaning. Listening to the situation in reflective distance enabled me to let go of my plans for the morning and to engage in another activity more in tune with what was happening. This spontaneous moment of distance proved to be a learning moment, fostering insight into my own reaction and ability to move with the unfolding situation. Moreover, in reflective distance, I found myself moving beyond my spontaneous annoyance and placing the situation in proper perspective: it simply was not the time to write. Becoming excessively upset about that fact would only have made matters worse. I had to respect and move with what was happening. As a result, I would have to wait for another time to continue writing.

Such flexible adaptation is not always possible. However, reflective distance does provide the necessary time and space to stand back from a situation in order to look at it with greater objectivity and to consider possible alternatives and choices. Thus we gradually grow into a sense of healthy and wholesome control over our lives, rather than allowing ourselves to be excessively controlled or enslaved by external events.

Standing apart from our outer world in reflective distance also enables us to bring an experience to closure. While we are present to reality, we try to remain open to its unfolding mystery. We allow life to emerge in all its freshness and fullness. But because of our human limitations, our ability to remain open to any experience is also limited. Just as we can listen to another person speak for just so long, so too are we able to listen to any aspect of reality for only a limited length of time.

Several years ago some friends and I traveled through Europe for two weeks. Since this was a once-in-a-lifetime opportunity, we decided to see as much as we could in that short time. We traveled from one country to another and from city to city, spending but a day or two in each. It was an exciting experience. However, as the last days of our whirlwind tour approached, I felt increasingly tired. At times I found myself saying, "I just can't look at another new place or thing!" I would rest for the better part of a day and begin to feel reenergized, ready to travel later in the day. However, in moving out to tour a city or visit a church, museum, or historical site, I once again felt exhausted. I had reached my saturation point. The pace had not afforded time to process experience, and now my exhausted self was telling me that I had no choice but to stop.

This same dynamic occurs on the everyday level. At times, our frantic pace allows very little or no time to reflect on our experiences and bring them to natural closure. Consequently, we may find ourselves feeling drained and exhausted because we have reached the saturation point of unprocessed experiences. Experience touches us, whether or not we wish. It seeks its own meaning and place within the context of our lives, whether or not we give it space. Reflective distance provides the time and space to listen and to allow meaning to emerge. In this way our daily experiences find their proper home within us.

On the morning I was trying to write, for example, I was present to the unfolding reality of various unavoidable interruptions. There was nothing I could do to stop them and, because of the circumstances, I could not escape them. In reflective distance, I was able to listen to what these interruptions were saying. The moment of closure occurred as I realized that this was not the time to write. In this realization, I was respecting in my own unique way the reality of what was happening. Closure, then, can be described as the moment of reaching a conclusion, however tentative, as a result of attentiveness to the revelations of a specific situation.

Closure represents the beginning of the integrative moment of experience. The meaning of any life experience, however insignificant it seems, becomes part of who we are. While enriching us, the meaning of our lived experience also touches the mystery of who we-are-not-yet, thus calling us beyond ourselves.[5] As we begin to integrate meaning discovered in reflective distance, we allow ourselves to be influenced and changed by it. In a unique way it becomes part of us. The meaning of the interruptions became part of me as I began to respect and accept it: this was not the time to write. I could have rejected or resisted that truth as I had on other occasions. However, I chose to respect it, allowing it to become part of my attempts to develop a listening presence. At the same time, the meaning of this situation called me beyond my feelings of annoyance and tension, beyond my sometimes inflexible self unable to change a plan. In that moment of self-transcendence, I moved toward who I-am-not-yet: the increasingly flexible me, able to respond gracefully to the unpredictable. The movement was imperceptible, but real.

Time is crucial to the integrative process. We cannot force ourselves to make the meanings of an experience our own. Rather, the process happens in its own way and at its own pace, as we begin to distance ourselves from our involvement. Our oftentimes superficial approach to everyday experiences prevents us from integrating any meaning we might discover. Programmed by our culture to focus on the extraordinary or the deeply meaningful, we frequently miss the subtle significance of our everyday experience. Reflective distance provides the necessary time and space to integrate experience. In the distance moment, we become aware of the just-noticeable differences, attentive to the subtle intimations of our spirit inviting us beyond ourselves. We allow ourselves to be touched and changed by even the most apparently insignificant meanings of ordinary life.

Jesus was well aware of the importance and necessity of stepping aside from experience. The Gospel of Mark tells us that Jesus sent his apostles two by two on their first ministry experience. For the first time they were going alone. They returned full of enthusiasm, sharing with Jesus all they had done and taught. Sensitive to their personal needs, Jesus invited them to "come by yourselves to an out of the way place and rest a little" (Mark 6:31). Alone and quiet, they would rest not only physically but also emotionally, psychologically, and spiritually. In this secluded place, they would not only share their experiences but also begin to uncover deeper meanings and significance. In quiet distance, they would begin to make sense of their days of intense ministry, to bring their experience to closure, and to integrate it into their lives. However, the apostles had so touched people's lives that it was impossible for them to get away. Men and women continued to follow them. Aware of the crucial importance of reflective distance at this time, Jesus would not allow them to forego this opportunity. He sought another solution. The gospel tells us that "Jesus and the apostles went off in the boat by themselves to a deserted place" (Mark 6:32).

This gospel passage stands as a reminder to each of us that we too need our out-of-the-way place. Reflective distance is not a luxury for those of us leading hectic lives and caught in the tension between superficiality and deepening. It is essential for all of us seeking to be true to ourselves and to God-in-us. In a moment of distance, however brief, we regain our bearings. We rediscover our perspective. We touch our inner selves. We are refreshed and reenergized, readied to meet the continuing demands of life.

Furthermore, such moments of distance enable us to give some direction to our lives. Rather than becoming prey to the shifting tides of feelings and reactions, to the opinions of others, or the pressure of authority, we need to step apart into a neutral zone where we can relax and breathe freely. There we begin to get in touch with our center, with the mystery of who we are. We become attentive to our barely perceptible inner resonances and dissonances. We perceive something of the delicate thread that holds our fragile lives together and gives them meaning. We begin to see how a specific experience does or does not speak to who we are. In reflective distance, we assume responsibility for our lives and destiny: whatever conclusions we draw or decisions we make affect the direction of our lives. In reflective distance, we become cocreators with God: our reactions and responses constantly shape and mold us into who we are becoming. Without reflective distance, we might unwittingly hand over the direction of our lives to outside pressures, and remain directionless, shifting with the tide of every passing movement. The power of our own feelings and reactions could enslave us.

However, opportunities for time and space easily elude us. We may find ourselves thinking, "I don't have the time." It is important that we begin to discover and uncover the moments that are already there—those distance moments built into our everyday lives. At various times throughout the day, we find ourselves walking up and down stairs, through corridors, or going from one room or building to another. We may find ourselves waiting in line, making beds, trapped in traffic, doing laundry, washing dishes, or drinking coffee. Perhaps we sew, fish, paint, or putter around the house or garden. At times, we may simply stop to catch our breath before moving on to the next activity. Occasionally we may find ourselves eating alone. Each day, we dress and undress, shower or bathe. We plant gardens and water them, mow the lawn, rake the falling leaves. We shovel snow or wash windows. Our days are filled with time when our mind is relatively free. These are natural moments of distance, precious opportunities to step aside from our usual activity in order to get in touch with our inner experience. They can be sacred moments of awareness when we are able to touch our enthusiasm or frustration; our concern or lightheartedness; our excitement or disappointment; our anger or peacefulness; our hope or discouragement. Such moments give us initial insight into our way of living through experience. We become aware of how we are touched and called forth. We begin to process our experience and to make it our own. Thus, in the moment of distance, the mundane material of our everyday lives is transformed into a source of enrichment.

Presence and distance deepened by Christian living

The mystery of the Incarnation lies at the heart of our Christian tradition. God's self-emptying in order to become human as we are human (Phil. 2:7) is a singular event in the history of humankind. It is the story of God's infinite personal love for each of us, a love so all-embracing that it is closer to us than the air we breathe, so infinite that it takes a lifetime to learn to surrender to it. This mystery of love defies intellectual comprehension: through it an infinite God has become accessible to us.

Jesus lived an ordinary human life so like that of the people of his day that they failed to recognize him as Messiah. After all, he was one of them, the carpenter's son—and nothing more (Mark 6:3). He was too ordinary to be the Messiah, fully immersed as he was in everyday life, just as we are. He had friends and enemies. He worked. He ate and slept. He walked and talked. He was gentle or firm, angry or happy. He could feel hurt, be sad and disappointed, love and be loved.

This Son-of-God-become-human, this Jesus who knows fully and intimately our human condition, invites us repeatedly to enter into a relationship of intimate love with him and with his Father: "Those who love me will be loved by my Father. I too will love them and reveal myself to them" (John 14:2). As broken, limited, and sinful men and women, we find it difficult to accept and respond to such gratuitous love. Just as the mystery of human love eludes us, so too does the mystery of God's love for us and of ours for him remain beyond our grasp. Only in faith can we enter into it and allow ourselves to respond to it.

The core of our Christian spiritual life, then, is the experience and life of intimacy with God and the incarnation of that life of intimacy in our everyday lives.[6] Intimacy implies moments of togetherness and of aloneness, moments of presence and of distance. Just as an experience of intimate presence on the everyday level spills over into a simple natural awareness of the loved one during periods of distance and separation, so too does the experience of intimate presence to God stay with us on the everyday level as a quiet and spontaneous awareness of him. As a result, our sense of the sacred dimension of our daily life is deepened. With Gerard Manley Hopkins, we cry out from the depths of our being, "The world is charged with the grandeur of God."[7] Immersed in the intimate experience of God's love, we grow in awareness of the manifestations of his love in the mundane experiences of our everyday lives.

Through intimacy with God, our entire being grows more deeply centered in him who is our deepest Center, more firmly rooted in him who is the Source of our lives. Our hardened hearts are softened to awareness of his touches of love in the everydayness of our lives. Our deafened ears are sensitized to hear his love beneath the obvious meanings of another's words. Our blinded eyes are opened to see his love in the ordinary. Permeated by his living love, our presence to life is enriched.

Furthermore, the distance moments on the everyday level become so many opportunities for touching the deepest Center of our center. Not only do we look at our feelings and reactions, or allow the meanings of an experience to emerge from the human perspective alone; rather, in faith, our feelings and reactions speak to us of God's movement in our lives. The emerging meanings of an experience are part of his ongoing revelation to us. Pauses, such as those described in the preceding pages, become so many opportunities to further nurture our love relationship with God. The distance moments open our eyes and ears to the imperceptible differences in our own feelings and responses. In the deepest sense, our feelings, desires, and responses become so many pointers of God's mysterious direction for us, and so many indicators of who we are called to become.

Thus our everyday rhythm of presence and distance is enriched by our awareness of God's living, active presence. Such an awareness surpasses our feelings and is beyond intellectual knowledge and understanding. It is a "faith-knowing" rather than an intellectual "knowing-about," an awareness deep in the heart of our being that radiates outward and takes flesh in everyday life.

Let us return to the example of the street described earlier. As I gradually allowed myself to become present to the street, I found myself feeling grateful to God for the wonder of it and for the creative minds of the engineers and architects. I was aware of the ingenuity of those who had invented the machinery needed to construct this street and for the strength and energy of the construction workers. All of these were his gifts given to individuals who in one way or another had contributed to this street. I found myself filled with awe and felt at one with the men, women, and children of the past, present, and future with whom I felt linked through the reality of this ordinary street. I sensed our oneness, not only as human persons but as brothers and sisters, sons and daughters of the same Father. I found myself walking up the street singing "How Great Thou Art." During those moments, God was very real to me. Even though I could not touch, see, or hear him physically as did the people of Jesus' time, he had become flesh for me that day.

Such experiences happen naturally and spontaneously, and cannot be forced. As our life of intimacy with God deepens and grows, these moments of awareness of his presence hold the potential of growing into an ongoing sense of presence. However, because of our humanness, we live with the tension between the self-gratifying and self-transcendent dimensions of our being. Consequently, developing an ongoing sense of God's presence demands personal effort: the constant discipline of moving beyond our natural apathy and laziness; our doubts and cynicism; our need to control and see results; our natural preoccupations and tendency to become scattered. The discipline of growing in awareness of God's presence calls for a gentle yet strong spirit-inspired effort that enables us to return home to our center when we are dispersed and preoccupied. It is the discipline of re-collecting ourselves and once again attempting to be present to the moment.

Various spiritual masters throughout the centuries have written about the discipline of becoming present to the rhythm of our breathing as an effective means of coming home to ourselves and becoming present to God. The anonymous authors of the fourteenth-century English classic *The Cloud of Unknowing* and of the nineteenth-century Russian classic *The Way of the Pilgrim* focus on this technique. The author of *The Cloud* suggests that as we quiet down and become aware of the rhythm of our breathing, we gather all our desires into a simple one-syllable word that is meaningful to us in our relationship with God. We are to repeat this word gently, to the rhythm of our breathing. Such repetition enables us to let go of recurring distractions, whether they be feelings, thoughts, or preoccupations. We thus allow them to be and gradually to fall by the wayside as we move more deeply to our center to encounter our Lord and Master.[8]

The message of *The Way of a Pilgrim* is essentially the same. However, whereas the author of *The Cloud* focuses on repetition of a word as a means of freeing oneself from distractions in order to move toward one's center, the author of *The Way of a Pilgrim* emphasizes repetition of the "Jesus Prayer" as a means of interiorizing the words and allowing their meaning to be ever more deeply revealed and experienced. The pilgrim, touched by the scriptural injunction to "pray without ceasing" (1 Thess. 2:17), sets out in search of a spiritual guide to direct him in the way of unceasing prayer. Having found one, he is encouraged to repeat with every exhalation, thousands of times each day, "Lord, Jesus Christ, have mercy on me." He is told that through this simple repetition, his heart will open to prayer; the prayer will become part of him, and he will come to live continually in God's presence.[9]

The methods described by these authors are simple yet challenging. We may tend to dismiss such works as written for another age—certainly not for our contemporary world. Yet, we need only step aside from our busyness for a few moments to get in touch with our deep yearning for the nourishment afforded by solitude and inner presence. Furthermore, the success of such movements as Transcendental Meditation, yoga, and mind control makes us aware that the technique of repetition is as valid and effective today as it was centuries ago. This technique is strongly rooted in our Christian tradition and offers a simple and highly effective means of growing in presence to God in our everyday lives. We are invited to take up the challenge, to use this method as a means of deepening our life of intimacy with God.

We do well to remember that such a technique remains simply a means of inner freeing, of centering, of interiorizing, of growing in awareness of God in the deepest core of our being. At home with ourselves and with God-in-us, we gradually become aware of his presence permeating various aspects of our everyday lives. A spiritual directee recently spoke of her growing awareness of God's presence in her life. Having met him in the depths of her being, she speaks of carrying on a "running conversation" with him throughout the day, expressing feelings, thoughts, preoccupations, and needs. She describes her growing ability to see her everyday experiences with new eyes and of being able to be present to God in and through them. She finds herself increasingly sensitized and deepened through the process. God is increasingly real to her.

Our intimate relationship with God is a mystery rooted in faith. Just as the mystery of human love depends upon yet at the same time transcends human effort, so too does the mystery of our life of intimacy with God demand the gentle discipline of our personal effort, yet remain a gift. He asks us simply to be open and responsive to his presence and movement within our lives. Brother Lawrence of the Resurrection, a seventeenth-century lay Carmelite, describes his efforts over a period of forty years to live in the presence of God in the midst of his daily activities. He acknowledges the importance and need of self-discipline, yet remains keenly aware that over and above his efforts, his ability to live in God's presence is a gift.[10] Like him, we are invited to enter into the way of firm perseverance in spirit-inspired discipline, while we patiently await the gift.

Many of us remember school days when we were encouraged to repeat ejaculations throughout the day. Perhaps we also remember stopping each hour for the "prayer of the hour." It is possible that these practices were taught us with very little explanation of the spirit behind them. Yet, as we consider the rhythm of presence and distance as the heart of developing a reflective attitude, and as we reflect upon the awareness of God's presence as the deepest reality of this rhythm, such practices take on greater significance. Their original purpose resurfaces: they were intended as pauses throughout the day that would call us back to the awareness of God's presence in the midst of our activities. Unfortunately, over a period of time these practices became routinized for many of us. Now as we rediscover ways of growing in mindfulness of God's presence, we can focus upon the reality to which such practices speak. We most likely no longer stop every hour to say a formal prayer, nor do we recite ejaculations. However, as lay Christians and as men and women religious committed to nurturing a life of intimacy with God, we are responsible to foster within ourselves a deeper awareness of God's presence in and through our everyday lives.

Mary offers us an example. From the heart of her being, she uttered her yes to the angel Gabriel. Her surrender was her wholehearted response to the unfolding of God's mysterious plan for her life. Its total demands were unknown to her: like us, she knew not where her yes would lead. Being human, Mary must have wondered and doubted, questioned and searched. At times, too, she probably failed to understand what was happening. Yet Mary was able to step aside to consider these experiences in reflective distance.

After the birth of Jesus and the visit of the shepherds, Luke tells us that "Mary treasured all these things and reflected on them in her heart" (Luke 2:19). Similarly, after her painful search for her lost son, and upon hearing his confusing response, she "kept all these things in memory" (Luke 2:51). In reflective distance, Mary allowed these strange and inexplicable experiences to speak to her. There she discovered meaning and inspiration, and allowed these experiences to become part of her, to strengthen her, and to nourish her intimate relationship with God. In reflective distance, Mary became more deeply aware of God's presence in and through her everyday experience, and more firmly rooted in his mysterious ways for her. Once again she reiterated her yes from the depths of her faithful heart.

Like Mary, we too are called to be present to our everyday experience—to own, treasure, and reflect upon it in our hearts. Thus we begin to develop a reflective approach to life. We grow in an awakened presence to experience and in the ability to listen to it. In so doing, we gradually get in touch with our own reactions and responses. We uncover hidden richness, and discover invisible layers of meaning beneath formerly meaningless experiences. We discover who we are and come home to ourselves. Gradually, we move toward a natural sense of God's loving presence in and through the ordinary experiences of our everyday lives. As a result, we slowly develop a sense of respect and reverence for the sacredness and richness of life.

1. See Douglas V. Steere, *On Being Present Where You Are* (Lebanon, Pa.: Sowers Printing, 1967).

2. Antoine de Saint Exupéry, *The Little Prince,* trans. Katherine Woods (New York: Harcourt, Brace and World, 1943), pp. 87-88.

3. See Thich Nhat Hanh, *The Miracle of Being Awake,* trans. Mobi Warren (Nyack, N.Y.: Fellowship Books, 1975).

4. Ibid., p. 9.

5. See Adrian van Kaam, *The Transcendent Self* (Denville, N.J.: Dimension Books, 1979).

6. See van Kaam, *Spiritual Identity.*

7. International Commission on English in the Liturgy, eds., *Christian Prayer: The Liturgy of the Hours* (New York: Catholic Book Publishing, 1976), p. 2058.

8. William Johnston, ed., *The Cloud of Unknowing and the Book of Privy Counselling* (Garden City, N.Y.: Image Books, 1973), p. 56.

9. R. M. French, trans., *The Way of a Pilgrim and the Pilgrim Continues His Way* (New York: Seabury Press, 1965).

10. Brother Lawrence of the Resurrection, *The Practice of the Presence of God,* trans. John J. Delaney (Garden City, N.Y.: Image Books, 1977).

Chapter four

Developing a reflective approach to daily life

"Life has a way of teaching us," said my friend. "A few years ago I worked about a mile from home. I decided that it would be good to walk back and forth to work each day. I needed the exercise. The fresh air would do me good. Above all, walking would solve a lot of car problems for others in the family. So, weather permitting, I walked to and from work. Most of the time I enjoyed it. It was a good break at the end of a busy day. But there were days when I almost ran home, driven by the million things I had to do when I got there. On those days that fifteen-minute walk seemed a waste of time. I felt as though I'd never get home!

"About a year later I was laid off for several months. I kept busy with family responsibilities and housework. I forgot all about walking. After a couple of months of being home, I began feeling agitated and preoccupied. I felt as though I were on a treadmill. My head was just too full and too busy. I didn't like the feeling. One day when I was feeling especially agitated, I stopped to look at what was going on. It suddenly occurred to me that I wasn't walking anymore. What came to me was that my walk to and from work had been a good settling-down time. It was a time to catch my breath and let myself quiet down. I decided to start walking again just to see what would happen but the opportunity for getting out was no longer there. I had to force myself to think about doing it. On some days taking a walk was the last thing I wanted to do, but I stuck it out. The strange thing is that within a matter of a few weeks, I was already feeling better. My head slowed down a bit. I began to feel more relaxed, and to realize how important that walk to and from work had been. It really had given me breathing space.''

My friend's experience speaks to the need we all have for personal time and space. The natural pauses described in the preceding chapter help to meet this need. However, because our reflective life needs ongoing nourishment, we must incorporate created pauses into our daily lives. These consciously created times enable us to step aside from our everyday busyness to allow ourselves simply to be. Created pauses differ from natural ones in that they are consciously chosen; that is, we attempt to discover and incorporate into our lives concrete ways of nourishing our reflective life. We must structure these pauses into our day, creating the necessary time and space. My friend did this by taking the time to walk.

Created pauses fall into two categories: those related to creating physical space and solitude, and those enabling us to articulate our inner experience. Such created pauses are necessary complements to the natural ones and help us to develop gradually the contemplative attitude pointed to in *The Little Prince:* "It is only with the heart that one can see rightly; what is essential is invisible to the eye."[1]

The need for space

Each of us at times experiences the need for space. We may express this need in various ways: "I want to be alone"; "I need space"; "Don't push me"; "Don't crowd me in"; "I need to be." The focus of our need for space varies according to our experience. After being in a crowd for part of a day, for example, we may simply want to be alone. After intense emotional involvement with another person we may need to process the experience. When we feel joy or hurt, or when we are dealing with some inner struggle, we seek space to make sense of the experience. Again, at certain times in our lives as God draws us closer to him, we may find ourselves wanting to be alone with him. Whatever our experience of the moment may be, there is within each of us the need for a space that is refreshing and restorative—a place where we can come home to ourselves and allow ourselves freely to be who we are. My friend needed space simply to quiet herself.

However, our natural need for space seems foreign to our contemporary world, which so highly extols the values of group support and togetherness. Our need for quiet also appears to be continually undermined by the noise-polluted world in which we are immersed. The need to be is alien to a culture dominated by the need to produce. As a result, we may have unknowingly overlooked our need for quiet space: the strident voice of our culture drowns out the murmur of our inner needs. Moreover, we tend to trust more readily the culture's values rather than our inner experience, which is not only unique and individual but may often be countercultural.

By allowing ourselves to be still long enough to listen to the timid stirrings of our inner selves, we discover that being alone is just as important as being with others. Being in quiet is as necessary as being in noise. Being is as vital as doing. In stillness, we discover that life is lived in the creative tension between aloneness and togetherness; quiet and noise; being and doing. There we discover that adhering to our culture's values has limited our growth and development, that cultural values do not foster a reflective attitude. There we become aware that our inner needs cry out to be heard and respected.

In quiet, we discover that at the heart of our being is a still center: a part of us, however small, that welcomes and needs peaceful aloneness.[2] At times, perhaps, inner tensions, pressures, and strains may be so overwhelming that we are afraid of being alone and quiet. We fear listening to and feeling our inner chaos. Or we may be so caught up in hectic living that we are frightened by the mere thought of being quiet and alone. At such times, silence and solitude are real disciplines. Yet, if we are intent on developing a reflective attitude, we must incorporate these elements into our daily life. Perhaps we can begin with a few brief moments each day during which we listen to quieting music, or take a walk, or allow ourselves to absorb the sights and sounds of nature. The silence of these natural experiences is nonthreatening. In the quieting, our spirit is touched and filled by the beauty that surrounds us. With time, this space grows increasingly comfortable despite what we may be experiencing on other levels of our being.

Retreating to our quiet center is not an escape from tensions, pressures, and preoccupations. Rather, we move through and beyond the immediacy of these concerns into our inner space where we can relax. Our concerns remain, but not in the formerly compulsive, preoccupying way. Now we can look at them with the objectivity of distance and in the calm of quiet. Gradually, we view them within the broader perspective of transcendent reflection, and allow them to take their proper place as the legitimate but limited concerns that they are. We may not emerge from our center with any solutions, for our inner space is simply a place to be and let be. However, we may feel calmer and more relaxed, invigorated and ready to deal with our concerns, which no longer seem so overwhelming.

In taking a consciously chosen, created pause, we are forming an outer physical space that will foster movement into our inner space. There, we dwell reflectively upon our experience, allowing it to speak to us and to fashion us into the persons we are called to become. In the distance of quiet and solitude, we reflect upon our reactions, not to chastise ourselves but to learn from experience. Our quiet inner space thus becomes a nonjudgmental place for growing in self-awareness and for redirecting the focus of our lives.

Finally, our center becomes the place where we can be with ourselves as we are. There we can risk removing our masks without fear of being hurt. We can simply be, without feeling compelled to prove ourselves by doing. Initially, we may feel uncomfortable with our real self, who may be something of a stranger. We may feel ill at ease with simply being. We may also be tempted to put our mask back on and rush back to our busyness. It is important to trust the process and to respect our pace; we have to be gentle with ourselves and yet at the same time challenge ourselves to remain alone. With time, we will begin to feel increasingly comfortable. Gradually we will learn to breathe freely and to relax. Imperceptibly we will come to know the stranger within.

A concrete example may help clarify this process. The directors of a recent workshop in which I participated structured our days so that a full day and a half of prayer preceded our discussion of the issues that brought us together. The procedure was simple. The leaders brought us into prayer, offering reflections and giving us a direction. We then prayed quietly for an hour on the suggested Scripture passage, and returned to share our prayer experience in small groups. This procedure was repeated three times, allowing a half-day for each session. Through quiet prayer, the facilitators hoped to slow us down, to help us to get in touch with our experience, and to meet the Lord within ourselves and in one another.

Early in the course of the first day, an intensely work-oriented woman expressed her frustration at the prospect of spending so much time in prayer. She wanted to be about the actual work. However, at the end of that same day, she exclaimed, "My feelings of frustration are gone. These sessions have been so good that I'm ready to spend the next four days in prayer!" Despite her frustration and resistance, she had trusted the process and allowed herself to be carried by it. As she encountered herself, her God, and other participants, her attitude was transformed.

Pivotal in her movement was the ability to trust the process. In the same way we are invited to get in touch with our personal need for quiet solitude and reflective space. We are challenged to create regular pauses, to trust the experience, to allow ourselves to let go of our ordinary way of being. We are invited to enter into the experience of solitude and to allow ourselves to be carried by it.

Such created pauses are a necessity. Without reflective space, we risk losing control of our lives and being controlled by life itself. We risk losing the richness of our experience and, consequently, something of ourselves. We risk losing our limited freedom, thus becoming robots in the midst of life. We risk losing our center and becoming fragmented.

> A life without a lonely place, that is, a life without a quiet center, easily becomes destructive. When we cling to the results of our actions as our only way of self-identification, then we become possessive and defensive and tend to look at our fellow human beings more as enemies to be kept at a distance than as friends with whom we share the gifts of life.
>
> In solitude we can slowly unmask the illusion of our possessiveness and discover in the center of our own self that we are not what we can conquer, but what is given to us. . . . It is in this solitude that we discover that being is more important than having, and that we are worth more than the results of our efforts.[3]

In the created pauses of quiet solitude, we come home to ourselves. We step aside from our ordinary pace and allow ourselves to learn from our experience. In this way we are refreshed and grow imperceptibly in a reflective attitude.

Expressing our inner experience

Another important means of developing a reflective attitude is learning to express our inner experience. Putting into words what we experience is, at times, difficult—especially at first. Initially our inner world may be foreign territory to us. It can seem a strange place if we normally live outside of ourselves, and we may tend to enter it hesitantly, fearing what we may or may not find. Becoming aware of our inner experience is a slow process and learning to describe it is equally gradual.

Moreover, finding the vocabulary to describe our inner world is sometimes frustrating. Written or spoken words often seem to fall short of our actual experience. At such times, an art form or creative body movement may better convey the depth of an experience that seems inexpressible. Or we may be able to identify with a certain piece of music or work of art that speaks for us. Again, we may find our experience best described in a book that touches us deeply.

Ways of expressing our experience are as varied as our human creativity, but all of them require taking the time to get in touch with what we are experiencing. This process fosters reflection: a bending back on what we are living. Two common ways to step back and reflect are journal writing and speaking with another.

Journal writing

As embodied spirits, we are in constant search of self-expression. Our actions and gestures, our facial expressions and body movements, our words and deeds, the creations of our hands—all reveal something of our inner selves and tell a part of our story. Journal writing is also a means of self-expression. It is a technique of re-collection by which we gather ourselves to ourselves in order to get in touch with our inner experience and to express its personal meaning through writing. The journal has been described as "a word and a deed, a collection of words and deeds of a self in dialogue with itself seeking to articulate its inner word and to embrace it."[4] Embracing our inner word, the uniqueness of who we are, means dwelling upon it in order to discover and uncover its meaning. To some extent each of us is a stranger to our inner selves. Because we live primarily on the conscious level, we fear how we will fare in the unfamiliar world of the intangible and the invisible. What will we discover there? Will we be able to understand and control it? How will we deal with what emerges?

Journal writing enables us to move through this unexplored world at our own pace and in our own way. Since the journal is an expression of our inner journey, there is no right or wrong way to do it. The primary guideline is that it describe and express our feelings, moods, and reactions to ordinary experience. At first we may not be readily in touch with "feeling" words, and our initial description of our inner world may be limited to such umbrella phrases as "I feel good" or "I feel bad." Gradually, familiarity with our inner experience leads to greater ease of expression. We become more discriminating: feeling "good" may mean that we are happy, alive, enthusiastic, peaceful, comfortable; feeling "bad" may mean that we are sad, depressed, angry, discouraged, tense. Initially such words may frighten us: we may find it difficult to accept the fact "I am sad." However, being able to put a name on our feelings, to own them as ours, is freeing. No longer does the uncomfortable feeling float aimlessly inside us; rather, we have made it real through writing. Once we have given it a name, it becomes easier to face and deal with.

It is also important that journal writing flow from our lived experience. Our everyday experiences are rooted in life. Our feelings and reactions emerge as our unique response to various life situations. We look at experience not to analyze or dissect it, but rather to get in touch with how we have lived through it, with what it is telling us about ourselves. At times, we may find ourselves being carried away by our feelings. When this happens we can lose touch with a specific experience and simply flow with our intense feelings. Or the experience on which we are reflecting may become distorted by an excessive emphasis on our feelings and reactions. Then we no longer are grounded in life but rather are introspectively engrossed in our myopic world of emotions. We have lost sight of our experience.

It is essential, then, that our journal entries be rooted in transcendent self-presence. We attempt, as much as possible, to place our feelings and experience within the broader perspective of a whole situation or event. By doing so, we can begin to see the relativity of what may initially seem absolute and over-whelming. In transcendent self-presence, we can acknowledge that for the time being we are bogged down by our feelings and unable to move beyond them. We learn to respect where we are, without judging or chastising ourselves, focusing rather on what we are learning from the experience. We realize that we cannot simply get rid of painful or uncomfortable feelings. Rather, we must patiently allow ourselves time to work them through. We become aware that through repeated expression of those feelings that seem to entrap us, we are imperceptibly being freed from their hold on us. Slowly they assume their rightful place within the total context of our lives.

In those moments when transcendent self-presence seems im-possible, we need to be compassionate and bear with ourselves. Occasionally, a feeling or a struggle may be so overwhelming that we cannot see or move beyond it: we are possessed by it. At such times we need to listen to and stay with the obvious. Fight-ing or trying to move elsewhere is futile. We may find ourselves spontaneously going to our journal two or three times a day simply to empty out what we are experiencing. As we continue to create the space to explore our experience, it begins to feel less overwhelming, and we are able to take a small step beyond it. With time we can allow it to be and focus on its meanings.

Someone once shared with me her own struggle to move beyond a deeply hurtful experience. For a long time she was overwhelmed by hurt, pain, and anger. She often began her dai-ly journal entry with something else, but almost inevitably found herself writing about her pain and expressing her anger. As the months passed and as she continued to write out her feelings, they became less intense. They were still there, but they no longer controlled her. As a result, she found herself needing to express them less frequently.

Gradually she could allow herself to get in touch with what she had learned from the painful experience. For her, this was a significant step in moving beyond her feelings. About a year later, while participating in a prayer weekend, she was asked to reflect on a death-resurrection experience in her life. Now, she could look at her own painful experience with greater distance and objectivity than ever before. As she contemplated its life-giving aspects, she found herself writing, "It was a small price to pay for so much growth!" At that moment she realized how far she had come: she now felt more completely freed and enabled to focus on the life that had emerged from overwhelming pain.

Her ability to persevere in the created pause of journal writing fostered movement and growth and enabled her to become increasingly reflective about an experience that initially had made no sense to her. She discovered life where there had seemed to be no life, meaning where there had been none, transcendence where she had felt trapped.

In order to be an effective means for developing a reflective attitude, journal writing must be done regularly. To write sporadically or to reflect on only positive or negative experiences fosters a one-sided awareness of ourselves. It is important that we create a regular time and space to write, preferably at the end of the day. We allow ourselves to get in touch with and to write what we are feeling in response to a specific experience that is present to us. Then we describe, as best we can at that moment, why we feel the way we do. At times, we may think that we have nothing to write about—until we begin to let go and enter into the process. At other times, a feeling or an insight may unfold over a period of successive entries. It is important that we grow to trust our experience and move with it, allowing it to unfold and to reveal itself in its own way.

One of the journal's greatest benefits is that it offers us a private and nonjudgmental place to get in touch with our feelings and reactions. At those times when we feel inwardly full, the journal is the welcoming space where we can freely empty out whatever we are experiencing and view it a bit more objectively. Moreover, rereading the journal after several months of regular writing can open our eyes to the movement in our lives. We discover patterns in our feelings and responses. We get in touch with how we are called forth by certain persons. We uncover our strengths and weaknesses and ultimately glimpse something of our hidden life direction as expressed in our everyday life.

For example, rereading our journal entries can make us aware of the kinds of situations that are life-giving or death-producing for us. We may discover patterns in the kinds of things that make us happy or angry. We may come to realize that compassion is a real value for us and one that we are called to live out in our everyday life. Again, we may see ways in which we allow ourselves to be manipulated and begin to realize our need to be more assertive.

Movement, direction, and growth gradually emerge from who we most truly are as expressed in our journal. Thus we assume increasing responsibility for our lives: we make decisions on the basis of our inner experience, taking into account our strengths and weaknesses as they appear in the journal. We are then less likely to be buffeted by the tides of popular opinions or fads. We are less likely to allow ourselves to be manipulated. And when we do fall into these sometimes subtle traps, journal writing can open our eyes and enable us to learn from the experience.

Moreover, the journal is often the first place where we feel free enough to express what we are experiencing. There we can allow ourselves to become familiar with a new feeling or insight without fear of what another may think. We can freely look at and explore what we have discovered. Then gradually we will find ourselves moving from the written expression of a feeling or an insight to verbal expression. Individuals in spiritual direction who keep a journal have often shared that for them, the journal is the first place where they put words on their experiences and feelings. They report that speaking about an experience after gaining some written familiarity with it seems less frightening.

The created pause of journal writing requires a gradual growth in the ability to move beyond our ordinary functional or intellectual response to life. Furthermore, journal writing demands that we slowly grow to trust our moods and feelings, which we often dismiss as being unimportant. Although getting in touch with and learning to trust them as ours is often difficult to do, we can learn only by doing: by becoming present to the genuineness of our emotions.

Becoming aware of our feelings and reactions helps us to move toward integrating our experience, which in turn leads to becoming actively engaged in the work of personal appropriation. We no longer move passively or superficially through experience; we become increasingly reflective about our life journey. We are led to the wellspring of our being and begin to tap the deep currents of our inner life.

Verbal sharing

Sharing our feelings and experience with a friend or someone we trust is also an important way of developing a reflective attitude. In speaking, we express some aspect of our inner world. A thought, feeling, or a reflection becomes real for us when we can put words on it. Once verbalized, it no longer wanders vaguely within us. At times we may find ourselves struggling to put a name on our experience or repeating it in various ways to clarify it. In this process we are thrown back on ourselves and are led to discover new and deeper meanings.

A woman I know had become aware of what she called her need to compete as she tried to verbalize thoughts and feelings that were troubling her. As she spoke, she said, "I don't know if that word really says what I'm trying to say. That's not quite it." Her struggle to put a name on what she had discovered as well as her facial expression indicated that the words she was using did not capture fully her new awareness. I invited her to stay with her experience and to continue talking it out. As she went on to describe what she was feeling, she found herself saying, "I need to be needed." A sense of recognition and relief came over her as she spoke those words. She had been able to put a name to an important insight.

In talking it out, she had given herself the time and space to become familiar with her experience: she described how the insight had emerged; she spoke of experiences that had reinforced that insight; she shared feelings related to this new awareness and the impact they had on her. She was hearing herself speak much of this for the first time. It was difficult and she felt uneasy. But in the process of sharing her experience, she was able to begin to own it. Now she could look a little more objectively at what she was feeling. She could allow it to be and begin reflecting on moving with her new insight.

In sharing our experience with another, we may at times find ourselves carried beyond conscious awareness, expressing new feelings or insights and wondering where they come from. Sharing with another enables us to grope, to search, and to explore, and encourages unreflected-upon experiences to surface. We are stepping into new territory where much may be revealed.

The woman described above had become consciously aware of what she called her need to compete. In sharing that insight she was carried beyond it. She began reflecting on and sharing experiences that had receded into the background of her awareness. Speaking out one experience led to the memory of another. Expressing one feeling allowed others to surface. Only in this verbalizing process was she able to make sense of her insight, which she could now comfortably call her need to be needed.

Finally, sharing our experience may be an important means of affirmation and support, both for ourselves and for the person with whom we share. We may also find ourselves challenged to further reflection, refreshed, or enriched. After such experiences, we return strengthened to our workaday lives.

The man or woman with whom we share our experience can also foster within us a reflective attitude. He or she can create the caring space that gives us the freedom to express some aspect of our life experience and feelings. The other receives our offering, listens to it, and offers it back again in a way that can lead us to further question and explore our lives. At times we may come to the sharing locked into our experience: new insights invite us to broaden our perspective and call us beyond ourselves. My friend Mary and I, for example, often share various aspects of our life journey with each other. Our topics of conversation range from the insignificant to the more personally meaningful. Over the years, we have supported, affirmed, and challenged each other. In the excitement of a new plan or project, I have learned to rely on Mary's practical sense to keep me grounded. When sharing some aspect of my spiritual journey with her, I have often been stretched beyond myself and invited to further reflection by her own contemplative approach to life.

In sharing with another person, we are affirmed and supported. We touch our limits and possibilities and we are called beyond ourselves to become increasingly aware of who we are.

Special ways of sharing our experience

In addition to everyday possibilities for created pauses, there are special ways of sharing our experience that also hold the potential of fostering a reflective approach to life. As we move through the journey of life, we may periodically experience the need for psychotherapy to help us work through specific problem areas. Or we may experience the need for spiritual direction as a way to foster deepened intimacy with God through the awakening of our spirit and the transformation of our lives into the graced persons we are called to be.[5] Although there are significant differences between psychotherapy and spiritual direction, both provide the created pause of a structured time and space so necessary for developing a reflective attitude.[6]

A competent therapist or spiritual director helps us to look at specific aspects of our life in relationship to ourselves, others, and God. We are invited to bend back and to take a second look at our complacent ways of living. In the caring space provided by the other person, in this instance a professional with a particular expertise, we are encouraged to explore, at our own pace, previously unfamiliar areas of our lives. We can look at our feelings, listen to them, and discover what they are telling us about ourselves. In the process we begin to question our taken-for-granted patterns. Thus we grow in the ability to trust our experience and to allow it to reveal various aspects of the mystery of our uniqueness and of our way to God. In the trusting relationship with the therapist or spiritual director, we are free to be ourselves in order to come slowly home to ourselves and grow in inner freedom.

Through this process of expressing our world and of being listened to, we become increasingly insightful and reflective about our lives. Often during a spiritual direction session, for example, a person will say, "I've never said this before" or "I've never thought of this before." The structured time and space of the setting awaken and sensitize individuals to their experience.

With time, this reflective attitude begins to move beyond the confines of the session. As this happens, individuals in spiritual direction come to a session sharing insights that have occurred since the last meeting. They develop greater ease in expressing what they are feeling or experiencing. They become increasingly aware of God's presence in the ordinariness of their lives.

Growth in this attitude is gradual and often is not evident to the person in whom it is developing. It is made up of countless just-noticeable differences that, over a lifetime, lead to an inner transformation and turning to God from the heart of one's being.

Although therapy and spiritual direction are special temporary means of fostering a reflective attitude, they nonetheless exert a powerful influence on our lives. As we enter into and move with the reflective process of these structured professional situations, we reach the point of no return; that is, as we attempt to remain true to the inner self we are discovering, we come to see that we can no longer return to our nonreflective way of living. Our inner self has been touched and awakened; our inner horizons have expanded and broadened. We are more aware of ourselves and more keenly in touch with our experience. As a result, reflection becomes a necessary part of our everyday lives. We may find ourselves needing to listen to our inner experience, to stay with our feelings, and to step back regularly from the immediacy of our everyday work in order to discover God's ways for us in it. We may spontaneously take advantage of life's natural pauses and seek opportunities for created pauses as we grow in awareness that our inner self is in constant need of nourishment. Imperceptibly, we approach life more reflectively.

The common ways of Christian living

The common ways of Christian living such as personal prayer, periods of silence and solitude, spiritual reading, and retreat are time-tested structures that foster within us growth in a reflective attitude. They lead us toward a deepened relationship with God. However, it is not sufficient that these common ways be highly encouraged by the Church or by the rule of an order or congregation. Nor is it enough for us to know that we need silence and solitude, prayer and recollection. In order to be effective, these common ways must become our own. We need to create the space for them in the here and now of our lives.

Taking the time to incorporate these practices into our lives remains an ongoing challenge. Preoccupied with our ministry as well as with the responsibilities and obligations of family or community living, we easily dismiss our need to step aside for a time. At such moments we would do well to call to mind the essence of our lives: as baptized Christians we are committed to center our lives increasingly on God, to grow in intimacy with him, and to incarnate in our lives and ministry our intimate love relationship with him. If not, we risk becoming "noisy gongs and clanging cymbals" (1 Cor. 13:1). Just as human love needs to be nurtured if it is to grow, so too does our relationship with God require nourishment. The common ways of Christian living constantly remind us of our call to incorporate these structures into our lives in a way that is realistically possible.

As contemporary Christian men and women, we often find ourselves bombarded by countless needs beyond our actual responsibilities. Our consciousness has been raised to issues of social justice. We have become acutely aware of the poor who surround us. The media have helped heighten our awareness of countless problems throughout the world. We are urged to keep informed, to take stands on various issues, and to become involved in living gospel values in a secularized society. Furthermore, we may often be called upon to meet various parish or neighborhood needs over and above our already demanding family, community, and professional responsibilities.

In the face of so many unmet needs, we sometimes feel guilty that we are not doing more. To ease our guilt, we may become overinvolved and unable to say no. As a result we run from one place to another while carrying the pressure and tensions of one activity to another. Fragmentation results. Caught in a whirlwind of obligations, we may feel that we cannot let go of any of them. We find little time to create the space necessary to nourish our relationship with God. Thus we risk becoming emptied of him whom we profess to serve and emptied of his love which we attempt to bring to others. We risk becoming hollow as well as burned out.

The needs we see around us cannot be minimized: they touch us and call for a response. However, a genuine response can come only from a heart in touch with its Source, and in dialogue with its individual possibilities and limitations. In the quiet of our center, we touch our deepest Center. Within the horizon of faith, we discover that God alone can truly refresh and restore us. We regain our perspective and come to see God as the source of our service to others. His ways and values must increase while we must die increasingly to our willfulness. We discover the space to take a long hard look at Jesus, whose human life was confined to Nazareth and the surrounding villages. He, like us, was limited by time and space. He too was aware of the countless needs of his day. Like us, he attempted to respond to these needs. He, too, must have felt frustrated by his inability to reach more people. The Savior of the world was confined to a few villages in a small nation oppressed by a foreign power. And yet Jesus could be at peace with these limitations because the eyes of his heart remained firmly fixed on his Father and on the ongoing revelation of the Father's will for him. Rooted in that will, he could accept the limitations of his ministry. For him, such acceptance became part of his redemptive mission. He had come not for his own glory but to reveal his Father.

As we struggle with endless calls to Christian service, we do well to reflect on our motivation. Do we find ourselves wanting to save people? Are we motivated by our compulsive need to be busy with many things? Do we fear moments of quiet and aloneness? Are we seeking to ease our guilt? Are we looking for affirmation and acceptance? Are our decisions regarding Christian ministry and service rooted in self-presence before God and his ways for us? Have we sufficiently considered our existing responsibilities and commitments? Have we looked at our personal possibilities and abilities? Like Jesus, we are invited to make peace with our limitations as part of our redemptive sacrifice for those we would like to serve but cannot. We are called to respect and to be purified by those limitations, that God's love may be revealed more effectively in and through the small areas of ministry and service that we can undertake. Such respect, acceptance, and peace come only as we create the necessary pauses to enter into our center and there to refocus the eyes of our heart on God within us.

For those of us engaged in active ministry, whether lay or clerical or members of orders, created pauses are precious times that cannot be omitted or set aside. They are slowed-down times of reflection and personal encounter with God which remain essential if we are to approach our everyday activities with any degree of reflective awareness. We may come away from prayer and reflection feeling as though nothing has happened and wondering if it has been worth the time and effort. Yet we have probably learned from experience that these oasis moments, however dry they may seem, do indeed nourish us. Perhaps we are a bit more reflective and a little more aware of God's presence in the midst of life because we have taken the time to encounter him in the quiet stillness of prayer. We may also know from experience that consistent failure to return to our center also affects our day: we get bogged down, unable to take advantage of the natural pauses, and end up being controlled by our busyness. Listening to such experiences fosters a deeper awareness of our need to create time and space for presence to God.

In addition to quiet and solitude, the common ways of Christian living also offer us opportunities to express our faith. Just as describing our everyday experience fosters growth in a reflective attitude, so too does sharing our experience of faith enable us to become more reflective about our relationship with God and his movement in our lives.

The Liturgy of the Eucharist and of the Hours offers us concrete daily opportunities for reflective encounters with God and with one another. These official prayers of the Church community are precious times for stepping aside from our activities in order to enter into the sacred time and space of a communal liturgical celebration. We are invited to listen to God's word as expressed in ritual. We receive his word into ourselves and allow it to reveal its personal meaning for our lives. We are encouraged to respond not only through the official words of worship but from the very depths of our heart. We are urged to participate by entering into the mystery of the celebration with others and by being present to one another as members of a worshiping community bound together by the oneness of our life in Christ.

Chances are that often nothing speaks to us in any significant way during these celebrations. However, our attempt to enter into communal worship is itself a reminder of God's living presence in the midst of our contemporary world. In a materialistic culture the liturgy stands as a reminder that something more exists: a transcendent dimension touching and calling forth the best of who we are. We can leave the liturgy strengthened by the supportive presence of others and encouraged to continue to live in our everyday lives the mystery that has brought us together.

A further way of expresssing our faith experience is through faith sharing. Many of us are probably familiar with some form of Scripture sharing: reflecting prayerfully on a Scripture passage and then sharing with others something of what has emerged for us.[7] As we reflect on God's word, it takes root in our heart. There we dwell on it and allow it to reveal its richness. The word we share with others, however simple, becomes God's word newly spoken in and through the unique individuals we are. In speaking our personal word, we make it concrete not only for others but for ourselves as well. At times we may find that our shared reflection goes beyond our original prayer experience. The reflective process, then, continues in and through our self-expression. The word is more firmly rooted in our hearts. Its meaning continues to be revealed.

We grow in a reflective attitude as we attempt to be openly present to the shared word of others in the group. While we listen we may be touched by how the same Scripture passage has spoken to another. Or we find ourselves challenged, inspired, and spurred on to further reflection by the word revealed to and expressed by another. In such sharing, God's word breaks open in a fresh way.

Through such sharing we are strengthened. We offer to one another the strength of our supportive presence along our journey of faith. We touch something of the mystery of ourselves and of one another. We glimpse the hidden beauty beneath a sometimes unattractive surface. We come to know others as deeply committed to God and God's people. We grow in faith in our God, who has gathered us together and who remains present to us in one another.

Relaxed fidelity to the common ways of Christian living according to our personal rhythm and needs fosters within us a reflective approach to daily life in its deepest sense. As God becomes more real for us in the encounter of prayer and reflection as well as through the expression of our faith experience, awareness of the divine permeates our everyday lives. The sense of God's presence transforms our perception of everything. All of creation truly becomes a gift of love. Our activities become so many opportunities to grow in awareness of God's presence. He accompanies us on our journey and is sensitive and responsive to our needs while at the same time challenging us to further growth and awareness. Christ becomes the friend who walks by our side listening to our story and enabling us gradually to change our focus from ourselves to him. As we listen to him, our hearts burn within us, our vision is transformed, and we come to a recognition of his presence with us (see Luke 24:13-35).

One day as Jesus walked by, John the Baptist pointed him out to two of his disciples. They in turn left to follow Christ. Aware that he was being followed, Jesus asked them, "What are you looking for?" To the disciples' question, "Rabbi, where do you

stay?'' Jesus invited them to "come and see." Of this encounter
the gospel says, "They went to see where he was lodged and
stayed with him that day" (John 1:35-39). The common ways of
Christian living are Jesus' way of extending a similar invitation
to each of us: "Come and discover where I am for you. Come
apart in quiet prayer and solitude and enter into your heart.
There I will reveal myself to you and draw you into my own
heart. There you will discover new life and space. Your vision
will broaden and you will return to your everyday life transformed and strengthened by a deepened awareness of my personal love for you. Yes, come and see and in that experience surrender to my loving ways for you. Come to know me as your
God, intimately involved in your everyday life and concerns.
Come and see—and discover the one for whom your restless
heart searches."

Like the apostles who emerged from their "come and see" experience enthusiastically telling their friends, "We have found
the Messiah!" (John 1:41), we too leave our own "come and
see" moments energized and enlivened. We soon realize that we
proclaim the Lord in and through our being, for as we create
time and space to be with him, we are led into a deepened intimacy that transforms our life and spills over into our everyday
relationships and ministry.

1. Saint Exupéry, *The Little Prince,* p. 87.
2. For further elaboration of the need and benefits of quiet and
solitude, see Maxwell Maltz, *Psychocybernetics* (New York: Pocket
Books, 1969), p. 193.
3. Henri J. M. Nouwen, *Out of Solitude: Three Meditations on the
Christian Life* (Notre Dame, Ind.: Ave Maria Press, 1974), pp. 21-22.
4. George F. Simons, *Keeping Your Personal Journal* (New York:
Paulist Press, 1978), p. 11.
5. Carolyn Gratton, *Guidelines for Spiritual Direction* (Denville, N.J.:
Dimension Books, 1980), pp. 83-94.
6. I do not wish to overlook or minimize the significant differences between psychotherapy and spiritual direction. I simply wish to consider

these disciplines as means of fostering a reflective approach to everyday living. Since my professional experience is in the area of spiritual direction, the examples used in this section are related to the latter. In doing so, I do not intend to minimize the benefits of psychotherapy. For a detailed study of the similarities and differences between psychotherapy and spiritual direction, see Gratton, *Guidelines.*

7. In sharing any aspect of our inner experience with a group, it is important that we respect our personal sense of privacy and that our level of sharing be determined by prudence as well as by our degree of comfortableness with others in the group.

Chapter five

The transforming power of reflective living

Some time ago, friends I was staying with returned from the garden with four green celery worms. We carefully placed them in a large gallon jar in which we tried to re-create their natural environment of twigs, celery leaves, and moisture. Our worm friends seemed to adapt readily to their new environment and began crawling around almost as soon as they were placed in it. A few days later I noticed that one of the caterpillars was agitated. I stopped to watch it crawl restlessly up, down, and around the jar. Not knowing much about the behavior of such creatures, I was puzzled. In my attempt to help I sought a few larger branches and placed them inside the jar. I thought the worm might need more than the small twigs we had gathered. I also replenished the supply of celery leaves. Perhaps it is hungry, I thought. A few hours later I returned and, much to my relief, found that the worm had settled quietly on one of the larger branches.

The next morning I was amazed to see that the caterpillar had shed its skin and begun spinning its cocoon. It was almost as if in its restlessness it had been resisting the process of change and transformation, however natural that process was. In the days that followed, we observed two of the other caterpillars undergo the same process: restlessness, quieting, shedding of skin, formation of the cocoon. The fourth caterpillar died before forming a cocoon.

None of us knew how long this cocoon stage would last. Although there were no observable changes in them, we knew that there was life inside each cocoon: the unattractive caterpillars were being transformed into beautiful black swallowtail butterflies. We could do nothing to rush the process. We had to wait. We did know, however, that an emerging butterfly needs to dry its wings in the sun. Again, in an attempt to reproduce the natural environment, we carefully placed the cocoon-laden branches in a small box covered with a screen and held down by a rock. We then put the box in a protected area of the yard, hoping to be surprised one day by new life. Much to our dismay, the box and its precious contents were blown away days later by a storm. We never caught even a glimpse of our butterflies.

Despite my disappointment, this experience reminded me of the process of human transformation. Just as each caterpillar was destined by its nature to be transformed into a butterfly, so too is each of us called to be transformed into the unique individual we most deeply are. For the caterpillar, the transformation process is a matter of weeks; for us, it is a lifetime process. Like the caterpillar, we often resist the process and are unwilling to let go of the security of the familiar. We often prefer embeddedness. In an attempt to maintain our comfortable ways, we become agitated and caught up in the resistance of busyness—a familiar defense against the intrusion of the new and unknown. Unlike the caterpillar, forced by its nature to move through the transformation process, we have a choice. As relatively free beings, we may choose to move through our resistance in order to respond to the process.[1] Thus we promote our ongoing growth into individuality. Or we may choose to continue to resist the process, thus unwittingly settling for a stagnant life.

The ongoing process of human transformation is an invitation to wait. Just as the cocoon stage of the metamorphosis process cannot be rushed, so our transformation cannot be forced or hastened. Learning to wait is foreign to our inclination to seek immediate results. Furthermore, becoming involved in the process demands taking a risk. It requires stepping back, letting go of our need to do and to control. We are asked simply to remain open to the process and to respond to it in whatever way is possible.

Trusting the process is critical. Like the cocoon, which remains the same for many days with no visible change, we often progress slowly. It is then that we become disappointed and disheartened because nothing seems to be happening. Yet the miracle occurring within the cocoon occurs also within us: the imperceptible change of each moment and of each day; the just-noticeable differences evident to the sensitive heart attuned to the mystery of human unfolding. For those open to life, an ongoing miracle continues to take place. We remain unaware of it until one day we find ourselves responding differently to a familiar person or situation. In those breakthrough moments, the butterfly of new life has emerged from the cocoon of our familiar everyday selves. Once more our experience makes us aware that trusting the inner process has borne fruit.

Our ongoing openness and responsiveness to life through a reflective attitude has a transforming effect on our entire being. Through reflection we come to perceive something of the mystery we most deeply are. We allow this mystery to emerge, to touch and speak to us: the unique name by which we have been called from birth begins gradually to inform the other levels of our inmost selves. Thus, over a lifetime we move toward becoming ever more completely and thoroughly formed by the wonder of our uniqueness. We are transformed from within by a continuous process which reaches fulfillment in the ultimate transformation of physical death and new birth into the fullness of eternal life.

Throughout the preceding pages, we have touched upon the transforming effects of a reflective approach to everyday life. In this chapter we will focus primarily on two aspects of this transformation: centeredness in one's being and awakening to life.

We will then consider the transforming effects of a reflective attitude on our Christian life.

Becoming centered in one's being

Growing in the ability to be reflective about our lives moves us gradually to the center of our beings.[2] We become increasingly familiar with our inner selves and feel at home in our inner space.

Because of our human limitations, it is impossible for us to live continuously and totally from our center. For the most part, our lives are spent moving in and out of our center. In moments and periods of centeredness, our perception is transformed. We are better able to distance ourselves from the immediacy of persons, events, and situations in order to reflect upon them from a broader perspective.

When we are reflectively centered within our being, our perception of another person, for example, is transformed. We start to see the other not only as one who agrees or disagrees with us or as one whose life-style we accept or reject but rather as one who is a mystery beyond our rational comprehension and control. The other person, too, is limited and struggling—just as we are. Dwelling in our center, we experience a sense of respect and reverence for the other. This does not mean that we agree with everything another says, nor does it mean that we necessarily accept everything he or she does. Rather, it means that we slowly learn to see beyond words and actions: we can accept the person of others while perhaps disagreeing with their behavior. We can respect and accept them precisely because of our reflective awareness that we share the same human condition.

Our emotions may at times prevent us from moving to our center. Feelings of hurt or bitterness, of jealousy or rejection, of anger or impatience may be so strong that we cannot see beyond them. We may find ourselves reacting impulsively or defensively rather than responding reflectively. We may become distant and unable even to face the other. When this happens, we need to move, as much as is possible, toward the inner space of our reflective center. There we allow ourselves the necessary time and space to gain distance from our feelings. There we can learn to face and accept these feelings as ours, realizing that there is nothing we can do to prevent their spontaneous upsurge. With time and continued reflection, we learn much about ourselves, the other, and the situation as a whole.

At times we simply cannot work through our negative feelings. Certain relationships and situations may remain temporarily or even permanently problematic. When this happens, our reactions remind us that we are human; that is, we remain ever on the way toward a reflective integration of experience and on the way toward trying to live relaxedly from the center of our being.

The centeredness resulting from a reflective approach to daily life leads also to an increased sense of inner solidity and strength. Our inner center becomes the firm anchor that keeps us from straying and becoming lost. When the storm rages and we find ourselves overwhelmed by intense feelings or absorbed in the busyness of our many projects and responsibilities, the strong anchor of our center calls us back home. There, we distance ourselves and gradually regain our bearings.

More solidly rooted in a healthy awareness of our strengths and weaknesses, of our possibilities and limitations, we grow in the ability to make decisions from within. We discover the strength to live with the consequences of our decisions. We do not overlook the opinions and insights of others nor the various aspects of the situation in which we find ourselves. Rather, we take these elements within ourselves and allow them to speak. In our center, relatively free of our overwhelming feelings and excessive compulsiveness, we allow ourselves to be present to our situation as it is. Decisions made at that level respect our personal uniqueness and are rooted in the concreteness of our life.

Such decisions are life-giving. When unfolding events reveal to us that we have made a wrong decision, we can remain relatively at peace: we know that inasmuch as was possible our decision came from our inner center in dialogue with the limited aspects of the situation of which we were aware at the time. We experience the strength to admit our mistake or failure and to redirect our lives.

The inner solidity and strength of centeredness are not the same as stubbornness or willfulness, which emerge from our compulsive self's intention to have its way at all costs. When we engage in such stubbornness, our vision is narrowed to the level of our willful plans and projects. Blinded by our compulsion, we may even fail to consider our own possibilities and limitations. Failing to dialogue with our concrete situation, we become excessively tense. Under the guise of being self-assertive and decisive, we refuse to bend to the demands of life. We refuse to listen to the opinions of others. We refuse to acknowledge the reality of who we are. Decisions emerging from stubbornness and willfulness are characterized by blindness, deafness, tension, and anxiety. Our growth is stunted and we become the victims of our inflexible self.

The inner solidity and strength of centeredness are rooted in our reflective presence to life experiences and are characterized by a sense of peace and harmony which flows from our efforts to be true to who we are. We are freed from excessive outer pressure and exert a healthy control over our lives.

Consider the following example. Shortly after making public her decision to leave religious life, Michelle unexpectedly lost her job, in which she had found much fulfillment and happiness. The surprising news came as a shock. She felt deeply hurt and angry. To lose her job was the last thing she needed at a time when almost every aspect of her life was changing. With its loss, she felt stripped of all that had been familiar. In panic she began the tedious process of job hunting. One day as we spoke, she said, "Every once in a while I find myself thinking, 'All you have to do is reverse your decision and stay in religious life. Then you'll have a job and a place to live. You won't have to go through all of this turmoil.' It's a thought that surfaces when I feel desperate. I cannot consider it seriously, though, because I know in my heart that I cannot reverse my decision and be at peace with myself. Sometimes changing my mind seems like an appealing solution. But I know that I can't do it even though I feel crushed."

Michelle's ability to remain faithful to her inner truth in the midst of pain was a result of her reflective life. Over the years she had learned to distance herself from the immediacy of experience in order to dwell reflectively upon it. In her attempts to live a centered life, she had discovered inner resources. She had begun to know a sense of inner solidity and strength which enabled her to move with her inner truth despite the odds. Now she was learning experientially that being faithful to herself meant living with the consequences of her decision. Her reflective approach provided her with the resources to move through this difficult period in her life.[3]

Awakening to life

As we develop a reflective approach, we are shaken out of our sleepy complacency. We are awakened to the dimension of mystery in the most insignificant aspects of our everyday lives. We slow down and learn to stop, look at, and listen to our everyday experience. Slowing down makes us neither less effective nor less efficient but rather enables us to return to daily life with freshness.

Rooted in a reflective attitude, we learn to approach life not only with our head but also with our heart. We become increasingly awakened to every aspect of life: its beauty and pain, peace and violence, love and hatred, liberation and oppression, joy and suffering, tenderness and harshness. Nothing leaves us untouched. Awakened to life we are open to learn from it and to allow ourselves to be shaped and molded by its mystery. Our hearts are increasingly attuned and responsive to the rhythm of growth, movement, and life in which we participate.

As we allow this to happen, our vision is transformed: the familiar world remains yet we see it somewhat differently. The seeing of the heart characteristic of a reflective approach sensitizes us to the sacredness of the mundane aspects of everyday existence. Awakened from our natural sleepiness we are opened to the invisible meanings present within our experience each day. Our reflective presence enables us to stay with and dwell upon these emerging meanings, which gradually become integrated into our everyday life. The ordinary begins to speak in extraordinary ways. We may, for example, discover that we have become more gentle in our way of handling tools, dishes, books, cleaning equipment, and so forth. We may find ourselves stopping to listen to the birds or the wind in the trees. We may become aware of a growing ability to listen to another with the ears of our heart. We may come to realize that we do our daily work with an increased sense of care. Peace and calm follow. Through a reflective presence we have been awakened to the sacredness of these various everyday realities. As a result, our seeing, hearing, doing, and touching are transformed. We touch and penetrate the heart of life—the sacredness of our ordinary daily existence and interaction with the world.

Perhaps one of the greatest benefits of being awakened to life is our growing ability to become rooted in reality. Each of us lives with dreams and fantasies of what we would like our life to be. Furthermore, each of us is more or less consciously motivated by countless "shoulds" and "oughts" around which we build an ideal of who we would like to be. Often such dreams, fantasies, and ideals may be a way of escaping something we cannot accept. They pull us away from our real situation only to blind us further to the life present beneath pain and struggle.

Being awake is an invitation to accept and learn from our life situation whatever it may be. Yes, being awake means that we will feel pain and hurt, but they are only one side of life. If we dull ourselves to these harsh feelings, chances are that we will also miss some of the joy and happiness of life. We experience life's pleasures only if we are awake to its hurt, pain, and disappointments as well. To be awake to life through a reflective presence means that we are open to receive and accept whatever life brings our way, knowing that our various experiences are all essential shades of the multicolored mystery that is our life.

As we awaken to life and become experientially aware of its mystery, we develop the ability to move flexibly with life and to respond to it in the limited way that is possible for us. We let go of our need to control and to be in charge, and allow ourselves to be led by the unfolding mystery in which we are involved. This does not mean that we sit back passively and let life take its course. We have the obligation to plan and organize as well as to be creative. However, as individuals rooted in a reflective attitude, we are invited to carry out our everyday activities inspired by reflective self-presence and openness to life. Thus, our plans and creative tasks are enriched by an awakened presence that allows us to adjust and modify our projects according to the ever changing demands of life.

The image of the rose comes to mind in this context. The rose simply is. It serves no functional purpose and is only there for us to enjoy. The rose begins as a bud that unfolds layer upon layer of petals. The process cannot be hastened. The delicate unfolding speaks of patience, respect, and letting be. We step aside, watch, wait, and allow it to happen. As the rose unfolds it grows in beauty until its center is revealed—the center from which each of the petals radiates. Then the rose reaches its peak. It is open, alive, awake, and centered. It is there for us to enjoy and admire. To each of us it speaks its message of life: "My life began as a bud, just as yours. I grew and blossomed in response to the world around me: the moist earth, the gentle rain, the storms and wind, the warm sunshine, the cool nights, the painful pruning, and finally the fertilizing. I have had to be awake to these elements and processes, otherwise I never would have blossomed to become who I am called to be. As you admire me, see also that my unfolding petals emerge from my center. Without that center I would not exist. I would be a scattered collection of disconnected petals. Allow yourself to be, as I have done. Wake up to life around you. Allow yourself to be touched by your everyday experience and to unfold and blossom forth into the beauty that is yours. In reflective self-presence, discover the center that holds together the many disjointed facets of your life, making of them the unique masterpiece that you are. Allow that masterpiece to unfold gently and slowly. Allow the gift that you are to become a gift for others."

I am reminded of a two-year-old nephew, filled with the joy of living, for whom no stone along the side of the road is unimportant and who can spend long periods of time watching ants. He is filled with the wonder of discovering life. My sister's comments in allowing herself to be called forth by the wonder-filled exuberance of her inquisitive child capture the excitement of being awakened to life: "What a joy it is for me to rediscover the world through the eyes of my two-year-old." Would that each of us, through a reflective presence, could awaken in the same way to the transforming power of everyday life!

Transformation and Christian living

Our call to Christian transformation is rooted in our baptism. Most of us do not remember our baptism nor even the date on which we were baptized. Nevertheless, through that sacrament an important event took place: we became children of God. Our life was given meaning and direction, and we were committed to grow into a deepened awareness of the values and attitudes of Jesus. On that day the living God made his home in the heart of our being, offering us the guidance, enlightenment, and strength of his Spirit to enable us to live out our commitment.

Our baptism, however, was more than an event. It is a mystery of faith that engages us in a lifelong process of growing into the Christians God calls us to be. Each day God invites us to enter into the death-to-new-life mystery and to accept being-in-process as a way of life. Through baptism, we enter into the mystery described by Paul:

> Are you not aware that we who were baptized into Christ Jesus were baptized into his death? Through Baptism into his death we were buried with him, so that, just as Christ was raised from the dead by the glory of the Father, we too might live a new life. . . . This we know; our old self was crucified with him so that the sinful body might be destroyed and we might be slaves to sin no longer (Rom. 6:3-4, 6).

The death of which Paul speaks is death to the many unfree areas of our lives, obstacles to the awareness of God's presence within our hearts. However, he makes it clear that this mystery in which we are immersed is also an invitation to grow more firmly into the new self to which we have been called through baptism: a Christ-centered self. Thus, we are initiated into a lifelong process of transformation which involves allowing God to take possession of our total being. We are called to nothing less than a radical re-formation of our lives.

These invitations to transformation do not come through the spectacular or the extraordinary, nor do they come through visions and revelations. On the contrary, they are rooted in ordinariness: in disappointments, failures, interpersonal relations, inner struggles, sickness, obligations, and so many other experiences all of which are unpredictable. These are opportunities to die to aspects of ourselves that need to be graced and transformed by the loving touch of God. Such moments of death are pregnant with the possibility of new life and of deepened intimacy with the Trinity.

Just as reflective living opens us to the transforming power of our daily ordinariness, so it also makes us more readily available and responsive to the transforming presence of God in our lives. Rooted in our center, we come to see that he is already there, present as heart of our heart, life of our life. Our baptismal call is an ongoing invitation to raise to the level of conscious awareness the reality of God's presence within our being and within our everyday life. Only through a reflective approach to life can this transformation of consciousness occur, for as we allow ourselves to slow down and to be present to everyday life, we allow for the possibility of the awakening of our spirit and greater intimacy with the Spirit of God within us. As a result, our vision is transformed: rather than focusing on the merely human aspect of an everyday situation, we move through and beyond ourselves and begin to see the situation as part of God's mysterious unfolding plan for us. Thus, in reflective presence to God, the mundaneness of our everyday lives becomes the sacred bearer of God's ongoing revelation to us, of his ongoing call to transformation.

As the eyes of our heart are increasingly turned to God through reflection, and as our will is more receptive and attuned to his will, he becomes real for us in our everyday life. He is no longer "up there" or "out there" but rather is intimately bound up with our lives as friend, companion, lover, savior. We may not always experience the closeness of his presence, but in faith we believe that he walks with us. In reflective presence before him, our faith in that belief is nourished and strengthened.

Gradually the reflective awareness of his presence influences our feelings, attitudes, and perceptions as well as behavior. Imperceptibly the Spirit of God permeates every aspect of our lives. Thus we grow in a discerning attitude. At the heart of our being we look at our feelings and reactions, our needs and desires. We listen not only with the ears of our heart but also with the ears of faith attuned, inasmuch as possible, to the stirrings of the Spirit within us. There we gradually glimpse something of his direction for us and experience a sense of where and how we are called to move in fidelity to our inner truth and to the truth of God in us. Although we may often feel uncertain, hesitant, or fearful about a decision, we experience a sense of "inner knowing" and the strengthening peace promised by Jesus to those attempting to live in fidelity to his ways. Thus rooted in our center and in the awareness of God's presence there, we live open to the ongoing revelation of his ways for us. We are discerning Christians.[4]

A reflective approach to life and to our relationship with God fosters an authentic spiritual life. We become rooted in who we are and in an experiential awareness of who God is for us. Our spiritual life, then, grows and develops from within. We are guided not by rules and regulations but rather by fidelity to the truth of our being and to the truth of God-in-us. As a result, we attempt to remain faithful not only to the law but to its life-giving spirit. Our Christian lives become Spirit-inspired.

Our rootedness in God and in faith does not make us less human. Rather, we come to God in and through our human struggles, weaknesses, and emotions. In attempting to live in fidelity to our inner truth and to God's truth within us, we are not freed of our unconscious desires and feelings, nor of our drive for power, status, or success. We remain vulnerable to self-deception, blindness, and illusion. Aware of our human weakness, we need such safeguards as regular prayer, spiritual direction, and the supportive challenge of others. Developing a listening attitude and allowing the necessary time for moving toward decisions minimize the possibility of blindness and self-deception. Ultimately we know that we must move with our limited human insight. God works in and through our limitations.

Despite an inner sense of peace and harmony, we may at times realize that we have made a wrong decision. When this happens, we can find a degree of comfort in knowing that we tried to be open to God's ways for us. Such moments become opportunities to recognize our limitedness and our need for continued purification. We come to God aware of our brokenness and dependence on him. Living with the awareness of his presence within us, we are more open to learn from our failure rather than to remain depressed or excessively upset by it. We attempt, as much as we can, to remain focused on him rather than on ourselves.

God does not expect us to be perfect Christians. Rather, he invites us to live in reflective presence to him in a way that is possible for us. What is important is that we endeavor to integrate that presence into our daily life. Just as Mary gave birth to the Savior of the world, so we must allow his presence within us to shine forth in our life. We are invited to be the Good News to those we encounter each day. Christ lives in and through us. Our openness to, acceptance of, and respect for reality are our ways of bringing Christ into the here-and-now world of our lives. Thus the mystery of the Incarnation continues to be fulfilled in and through the limited persons we are. Incarnating Christ, then, becomes possible for us insofar as we gradually learn to live with him as our center. In the reflective solitude of prayer, the limiting darkness of introspection and legalistic observance gives way to the freeing light of transcendent self-presence and to a lived faith.

As we learn to live in Christ through a reflective approach to everyday life, we too can say with Paul, "The life I live now is not my own; Christ is living in me. I still live my human life, but it is a life of faith in the Son of God, who loved me and gave himself for me" (Gal. 2:20). Like Paul, we continue to live our human life, a life of peace and anxiety; of joy and pain; of weakness and strength; of sin and grace; of disappointment and fulfillment; of moments of brokenness and moments of wholeness. However, as we grow in a reflective attitude and move toward our center, our life becomes a life of faith: faith in the God who continues to walk with us each day; faith in that presence in and through our daily experience. Like branches on the vine we share his life (John 15:1-8). Just as the life-giving sap nourishes each branch, enabling it to grow and bear fruit, so the Christ-life in us continues to transform us from within. Our openness and response to his life-giving presence nourish and sustain us. Through him we grow, are strengthened, and bear fruit.

As Christians committed to Christ through baptism, each of us is called to respond to and at the same time to nurture the precious Christ-life within. In reflective openness to the transcendent meanings of our ordinary experience, we enable his life in us to grow and to influence our entire being. Our vision, attitudes, and perceptions are gradually transformed—often without our knowing how. Throughout the days, months, and years of our lives, we continue to be formed into the God who dwells in the heart of our being.

---

1. For a more extensive development of the phenomenology of human freedom, see William Luijpen, *Existential Phenomenology* (Pittsburgh: Duquesne University Press, 1969), pp. 186-260.

2. For an extensive development of centeredness and its transforming power in a person's life, see Karlfried von Durckheim, *Hara: The Vital Centre of Man,* trans. Sylvia-Monica von Kospoth (London: George Allen and Unwin, 1962).

3. For autobiographical accounts of the human person's ability to transcend and grow from the most inhuman situations, see Viktor E. Frankl, *Man's Search for Meaning: An Introduction to Logotherapy* (New York: Pocket Books, 1963), and Walter J. Ciszek with Daniel L. Flaherty, *He Leadeth Me* (Garden City, N.Y.: Doubleday, 1973).

4. I do not wish to minimize the importance and necessity of the formal process of discernment. My intention is to point out that Christians reflectively rooted in their center and in awareness of God's presence there are already engaged in a life of ongoing discernment; that is, they are living in an ongoing dialogue with their experience, with life, and with God in an attempt to discover God's will. The need for more formal discernment may arise at various times in one's life. The formal process, then, is facilitated by this already-existing attitude of discernment.

Affirmation Books is an important part of the ministry of the House of Affirmation, International Therapeutic Center for Clergy and Religious, founded by Sr. Anna Polcino, S.C.M.M., M.D. Income from the sale of Affirmation books and tapes is used to provide care for priests and religious suffering from emotional unrest.

The House of Affirmation provides a threefold program of service, education, and research. Among its services are five residential therapeutic communities and two consulting centers in the United States and one residential center in England. All centers provide nonresidential counseling. The House sponsors a leadership conference each year during the first week of February and a month-long Institute of Applied Psychotheology during July. More than forty clinical staff members conduct workshops and symposiums throughout the year.

For further information, write or call the administrative offices in Boston, Massachusetts:

The House of Affirmation
22 The Fenway
Boston, Massachusetts 02215
617/266-8792